The Sierra Club Book of
Weatherwisdom

The Sierra Club Book of
Weatherwisdom

Vicki McVey
Illustrated by Martha Weston

SCHOLASTIC INC.
New York Toronto London Auckland Sydney

Text copyright © 1991 by Vicki McVey.
Illustrations copyright © 1991 by Martha Weston.
All rights reserved. Published by Scholastic Inc., 555 Broadway, New York, NY 10012, by arrangement with Sierra Club Books.
All maps by Vicki McVey.
Printed in the U.S.A.
ISBN 0-590-20725-3

1 2 3 4 5 6 7 8 9 10   14   01 00 99 98 97 96 95 94

For Jesse

Contents

...very en-*lightning*!

1
Weatherwisdom

Do you know what a ring around the moon means, or a red sky at dawn? Do you know what will happen when an east wind shifts to the west, or a morning fog breaks up by noon? If you notice such things and can figure out what they mean, then you may be able to answer other questions, too. You might be able to tell whether or not it's going to rain on your picnic or clear up in time for the baseball game. Or maybe you can predict when school is going to close because of a big snowstorm.

Ever since there have been people on earth, it has been someone's job to figure out the weather. Some people read clouds or watch animals, and others use precise instruments, but weather is so important that, one way or another, we've always tried to find out what it's going to do next.

People who understand about the weather, no matter where they are or how they have come by their knowledge, are "weatherwise." They have developed their own wisdom about how weather works by paying attention to the world around them and by collecting different kinds of information. If you want to become weatherwise, you will need to do the same things.

A person who is weatherwise knows how to forecast the weather. In our culture, the most well-known weather forecasters are professional meteorologists who use space-age technology to help them make their predictions. But there are weather forecasters throughout the world who make accurate predictions without the aid of modern science and technology. These are often people whose livelihoods depend on understanding what is going on in the world around them. Farmers, fishermen, and sailors, for instance, are all weather forecasters.

Anyone can be a weather forecaster. In some parts of the world, knowing about the weather is so important that all the people who live there learn how to do it. These people gain weatherwisdom just like anyone else: by paying attention to natural patterns and figuring out how some of them work, and by getting weather knowledge from books, teachers, and other weatherwise people. Here is an example of someone who is learning weatherwisdom:

Puma, a twelve-year-old Native-American boy, lives 12,500 feet above sea level, near one of the highest lakes in the world. Long ago his people, the Incas, chose as their domain the high valleys and plateaus of the Andes Mountains, along the western edge of South America. For more than 500 years, the Incas and their descendants have lived around the shores of Lake Titicaca, developing skills to help them survive in their high-altitude environment.

One of the most amazing skills Puma's people have acquired is the ability to read weather. They discovered long ago that many of the patterns that influence seasonal weather take months to develop. They realized that if they could recognize the earliest stages of such patterns, they would know what was going to happen later in the season.

As they watched for signs that would help them forecast the weather, the Incas noticed that certain plants and animals seemed to react to changes in the environment long before people even knew they were happening. They learned that these plants and animals could be used as early warning signals for seasonal weather. The people could observe them carefully and, by watching them, figure out what kind of weather to expect in the coming months. This ancient knowledge has been kept alive among the descendants of the Incas and is still used today.

All Andean farmers are weather forecasters, but even among them Puma's father, Quispe, is known for his ability to read weather signs. He is so skilled in weatherwisdom that his crops, in spite of being grown in the cold temperatures and rocky soils of the high Peruvian Andes, are unusually abundant. Puma, working side by side with his father for much of his life, is learning some of the ancient skills of his people.

One afternoon, for instance, while they were working in a potato field near their adobe house, Quispe and Puma discovered a nest of *tacarari* eggs. *Tacarari* are large spiders that mate at the end of July and the beginning of August and lay their eggs about the time that farmers begin preparing their fields for planting. Puma's father had told him that if the *tacarari* eggs were dry and small, that meant it would be a dry year, and if they were large and moist, it would be rainy. The nest they found that afternoon held many large eggs, and Puma was glad of this sign of abundant rainfall for the growing season.

Tacarari eggs were generally thought to be a reliable sign, but they didn't give enough information to base important decisions on — decisions such as what to plant, and when and where to plant it. So today Quispe was sending his son, Puma, to Lake Titicaca to look for other important weather signs.

Puma loved the huge lake, and could hardly believe his good luck in being sent there by himself. He knew that his father was trusting him with a very important job, but Puma also knew that he would do it well. He prepared for his short journey by throwing a few handfuls of roasted flour into the peak of his wool hat and stuffing two biscuits made of *quinoa* flour into his homespun shirt.

As he got into the marshes at the edge of the lake, Puma found a stick that he could use for measuring. He was looking for the nests of a certain type of bird that lived among the cattails. He knew that these birds liked to nest over the water because during the cold months, the lake was often warmer than the air above it and would provide heat for the nest.

The birds always seemed to know if it was going to be a rainy or a dry year — if the level of the water would be high or low — and would build their nests so they would be safe. If the nests were too high, their chicks would freeze to death, and if they were too low, they would drown. So Puma was looking for some of the newly built nests to measure their distance from the water and learn more about the coming weather.

Puma quietly gathered *totora* reeds as he waded through the marshes looking for nests. The reeds would be used for making sleeping mats and baskets, and for repairing the roof of his family's house. By the time he finally saw a bird landing in the reeds up ahead, his feet were nearly numb from the cold water. The bird shrieked in fury when Puma invaded its territory, but Puma was able to get over to the nest and measure its distance from the water. He used his thumbnail to make a mark on the side of the stick.

There were five more marks on his stick, and a large bundle of *totora* on his back, by the time Puma was ready to start his journey home. He was glad to get back to dry land and eat his biscuits and roasted flour. The marks on his stick told the same story as the *tacarari* eggs: according to the birds, too, there would be a lot of rain that year.

On his way home Puma had the great good luck of finding the nest of a small bird called a *leque-leque,* and after studying it for a few minutes, he was able to add his own new piece to the weather puzzle he was putting together with his father. He knew that during years of severe thunderstorms, these birds would build small stones into their nests to protect them from hail. The nest he found was so full of stones that it looked like a tiny fortress, and though that wasn't good news, his father would take warning and do what he could to prepare for a season of thunderstorms.

Quispe was very pleased with Puma's work. Good news or bad, it was all important. Now Quispe would be able to make his plans for the growing season, based on the traditional weatherwisdom of his people.

Although the old and seemingly unscientific methods of the Incas might seem strange to us, they have been proved to work, and they show us how to begin to acquire weatherwisdom for ourselves. As you read and experiment, you will see that most traditional methods for predicting weather (including your own, if you discover some for yourself) are based on patterns that people see in the world around them. Patterns tell you that one event usually follows another in a predictable manner (for instance, that a wind blowing from the north is usually followed by a drop in temperature), but they won't tell you why. In order to know why, you have to understand the processes that create weather.

One reason that weather processes make sense is that they are part of a system that runs according to natural laws, like "What goes up must come down" and "Water flows downhill." You are part of the same system, and if you have ever fallen off a bicycle or gone tubing down a river, you know that you are subject to the same natural laws. In the next chapter you will learn more about systems, because that's where understanding weather begins. But first, here are some projects that will help you develop your own weatherwisdom.

Weather Journal

Since this book will be a journey into weatherwisdom, and it is always good to begin a journey with a journal, you can start by getting or making a small notebook for recording your own observations. Learning how to observe the world around you is the first step toward weather-wisdom. You can observe with your own senses: how the sky looked when you got up and went to bed; whether there was any *precipitation* during the last 24 hours, and if so, what kind it was and how long it lasted; whether birds outside your house were noisier or quieter than usual; and so on. You can also observe with the help of instruments (and you'll learn how to do that in the next activity). If you record your observations every day, pretty soon you will notice that the things you've been watching seem to happen in patterns.

Another use for your journal is to keep track of conversations about the weather. Do you know any weatherwise people? If you do, you can get years of weatherwisdom just by talking to them. It's worth searching for weather forecasters (are there any farmers, sailors, pilots, or fishermen in your family?) and asking them to share their experiences with you. Write down your questions and their answers in your journal.

———————— Weather Station I ————————

Some weather events are invisible, like changes in the temperature, pressure, and movement of the atmosphere. Such things can only be measured with the help of weather instruments. But it is simpler to make basic instruments than you might think, and, if you are interested, you can build a weather station in your own backyard. To help you do that, there will be instructions in some of the following chapters for building simple instruments. By the time you are done with this book, you can have a basic weather station.

WEATHERPROOF BOX. A few of the instruments will be kept outside and will need some sort of cover to protect them from the sun. The best protection is an open, weatherproof box, about a foot or a foot and a half square. Wooden or plastic crates work well because they are partly open on the sides and allow air to circulate through them. The box will be mounted on its side, so that its bottom will become the back wall. The best place to put the box is on the north side of a building (that's the shady side).

THERMOMETER. The one instrument that you can't make is a thermometer, so you will need to buy one or use one that your family already has. Fasten the thermometer to the bottom of the box; then when you hang the box, the thermometer will be on the back wall. Ask an adult to help you hang the box.

RAIN GAUGE. One outdoor instrument that won't go inside the box is a rain gauge. To make this instrument, all you need is a straight-sided container, such as a soup can, with a scale in inches that you can

either attach to it or mark on the inside. It is very important that the sides of the container be straight up and down, and that the container be placed or fastened where there aren't any trees, wires, or overhanging roofs above it.

Because the container needs to be removed and emptied each time you take a measurement, you'll need to make a holder that it can slip out of and back into without much trouble. One good place to fasten the holder is the side of a fence or fencepost, but be sure the top of the container, when it is in the holder, is above the top of the fencepost. Use wire or an unbent coat hanger to make the holder.

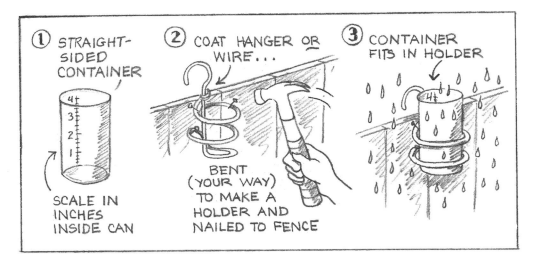

① STRAIGHT-SIDED CONTAINER

SCALE IN INCHES INSIDE CAN

② COAT HANGER OR WIRE...

BENT (YOUR WAY) TO MAKE A HOLDER AND NAILED TO FENCE

③ CONTAINER FITS IN HOLDER

Use a section of your journal for recording observations from the weather station. It's best to keep a daily record, and you can start now by recording temperature and precipitation figures. Below is an example of what a weather record page in your journal might look like. (You'll find out about barometric pressure, humidity, and other things in later chapters.)

DATE	TIME	TEMP.	BAR. PRESS.	HUMID.	TYPE OF PRECIP.	AMT. OF PRECIP.	WIND OUT OF	CLOUDS
2/20/90	3:30p	59°	LOW	HIGH	RAIN	⅛ IN.	NW	NIMBO- STRATUS
2/21/90	3:45p	61°	MED.	MED.	—	—	W	SCATTERED CUMULUS

2

A System Called Earth

All things that move on the earth — from bugs to hurricanes to you and me — are powered by the sun. This planet of ours, from the outer atmosphere to the inner core, is like a huge machine with billions of moving parts, and, except for heat energy from inside the earth itself, the whole thing runs on energy from the sun. One of the machine's most important jobs has to do with weather.

For thousands of years, weather was known and understood only in each small area where it happened. Nobody knew that our world is one complete system with all the parts connected, so that if something happened in one part of the world, it would sooner or later be felt in other places. People didn't understand, for instance, that brilliant sunsets in their own sky might have been caused by a volcano that erupted a month earlier on the other side of the globe.

But at the beginning of the Space Age, when we first traveled beyond our own atmosphere and saw Earth from out in space, we began to realize that our planet is one whole, huge system. The view from space caused tremendous excitement, but it also seemed to put us in our place. When we saw the earth from such a great distance, it became very clear that we humans were just a tiny part of the huge system.

And now that we have begun to understand how systems work, we have discovered that many things make more sense when they are seen as part of a bigger picture. Weather is one of those things. It is much easier to understand weather when we look at it as part of a larger system — and the system it belongs to, of course, is called Planet Earth. So let's take an imaginary journey into space, where we can see the system called Earth from a distance.

We'll go back almost 5 billion years, station ourselves beyond Earth's atmosphere, and picture a planet-sized ball of rock spinning in orbit around its young sun. From our imaginary position in space, we can see the system develop over billions of years as if it were happening in just a few minutes.

The planet looks dead: all of the raw materials for a system are there, but they're bound up in the rock of the planet. There is no water in its atmosphere, so there are no rain clouds swirling around it. You don't see any movement on the surface of the planet because there is no life, and it's hard to imagine that anything ever *could* live there.

The planet looks solid, but the rock on the surface is just a thin layer, and underneath that is a huge ocean of molten lava. From time to time you see eruptions of liquid rock spraying out into the sky, then dropping down and cooling to make strange formations over the land-scape. When such eruptions happen, *water vapor* and other gases that were trapped inside the molten rock are also shot up into the sky.

Eventually you see a swirling pattern of clouds around the planet

as these newly released gases gather in the atmosphere. Water vapor that is shot into the sky with the molten rock collects into clouds and then falls as rain. The rain begins to form pools on the rocky surface. After a few million years, the pools have become oceans, and a large portion of the barren planet is covered with water.

Although the planet now has oceans and the beginnings of an atmosphere, there still isn't any "air," and the system has a long way to go before it's ready for the development of life. But you notice that this new atmosphere seems to be in constant motion, and you watch the clouds form into swirling patterns that move over the surface of the planet.

One of the things you notice is that a wide band around the middle of the planet gets much more sunlight (and also heat) than areas near the poles. As you watch the patterns of the clouds, you see that the system is moving air and water from place to place and distributing heat from the equator (where there's too much of it) to the poles (where there isn't enough).

From time to time portions of the cloud cover are lit up from inside, as lightning discharges electricity within the atmosphere. The glowing clouds blink on and off, and this is such a strange and interesting sight that you move your focus in to see what is happening inside the atmosphere. As the gases are bombarded by intense *ultraviolet radiation* from the sun and charged with electricity by lightning, all sorts of different reactions are taking place.

The force of this bombardment breaks chemical bonds that have held tiny particles (called *molecules*) together, and from time to time these chemicals recombine to form different kinds of particles. The new particles are washed into the oceans, where they form a kind of thin soup that now contains the complex molecules necessary for life.

How this supercharged soup produces the first living entity is a huge mystery, but from your position out in space, two billion years after you began watching this ball of rock, you notice a patch of green floating on one of the oceans. The green patch is made up of billions of tiny bacteria-like organisms, and these organisms, the first form of life you've seen on the planet, have the amazing ability to produce food using only carbon dioxide from the atmosphere, water, and light from the sun. This process (called *photosynthesis*) is very important because, as it happens, water molecules are split apart, and oxygen is released into the atmosphere.

As oxygen begins to collect in the atmosphere, it gets bombarded by ultraviolet radiation and lightning, just as the earlier gases did, and new reactions take place. One of the most important reactions happens when oxygen gas absorbs ultraviolet radiation and produces *ozone*. After millions of years, as the tiny organisms on the surface of the oceans continue to release oxygen during the process of making food for themselves, ozone begins to accumulate in the upper atmosphere. A very thin layer of ozone forms a shield around our planet that blocks out some of the sun's damaging rays. Now all sorts of things are possible!

For one thing, with the protection of the ozone layer, plants can begin to move up onto the surface of the land. The first "pioneer" plants on the land have to struggle to survive on its rocky surface, but as the first plants die, they combine with rock grains and dust to form soil. It takes millions more years for plants to spread over the surface of the planet, but eventually more plants mean more soil, more oxygen, and more food for the higher forms of life that are beginning to develop on the land. Finally you are looking at the same living system that we see today in real satellite pictures beamed to earth from outer space.

Though all of the parts had been in place since the rocky planet was born, it took time for them to begin to function together: until the first organisms produced it, we didn't have oxygen in our atmosphere; until oxygen produced ozone, we didn't have a shield around our planet to protect it from the sun; until we had a shield, there couldn't be any life on the land surface of the earth. So the presence of plant-like organisms on Earth makes all other life possible. That's a good example of how a system works.

The system called Earth is almost 5 billion years old. In that period of time it has changed from a lump of rock spinning in space to the living world we know today. All the parts of the system — the atmosphere, the oceans, the land, and the raw ingredients for life — were contained within the original rock. Nothing has been added or taken away, so the air you breathe and the water you drink have been recycled for almost 5 billion years.

With the exception of an occasional meteorite, the only thing that enters the system is energy from the sun, and even that is recycled and transported around the surface of the planet before it is returned to space. Although some of the sun's energy hits the atmosphere and bounces off, and some is filtered out by atmospheric gases, most of it ends up being distributed throughout the system. Weather is the key to how that happens. Without the exchange of energy through weather, life on our planet would be impossible.

One of the most amazing things about the system called Earth is that all of the parts work together to maintain a balance. For instance, it is too hot around the equator, so the system shuffles some of the extra heat out to the poles, where it is too cold. This huge, ongoing heat-transfer project is taken care of by the atmosphere, which is one of the most important parts of the system. In addition to all of its other jobs, the atmosphere is where weather happens. In later chapters you will find out about the processes that create weather, but in the meantime, the best way to understand how a system works is to study one firsthand. Here's a project to help you.

———— Building a System ————

It is fairly simple to build a system that has all the components of Earth's system: an atmosphere, water, land, and living organisms. (Your system will eventually even make weather.) Because this project will take time and effort, it might be fun to build it with another member of your family or with a friend. Here's how to do it:

To begin with, you will need a large glass jar — the bigger, the better. Some restaurants still get food items (like maraschino cherries and pickles) packed in large jars, and if you ask at the right time, they might give you one. Another alternative is to buy a big glass container. Your jar will need to be closable, so get one with a lid. Depending on the size of the jar, you will also need one or several small plants (about two inches high) and some soil for them to grow in.

Many large discount or grocery stores sell houseplants (especially small terrarium plants) at very reasonable prices. If you don't want to spend money on your system, the process of building it might be more fun, but it will also take more time. Unless it is the dead of winter, you can usually transplant small plants from outside, or take cuttings of houseplants and root your own. The best place to find small plants outside is along the banks of streams, because these types of plants are used to lots of moisture and will do well in the tiny greenhouse you are building.

THREE WAYS TO GET PLANTS

① BUY THEM AT A NURSERY ② DIG THEM UP ③ ROOT THEM

PLASTIC BAG

3"

2"-3"

ROOTS

You'll need some kind of digging tool. A garden trowel, or even a large spoon, will work fine. Take some plastic bags to put your plants in. When you dig up a plant, cut all around it very carefully to a depth of 2 to 3 inches to keep from disturbing the roots. If you find a small plant with moss growing around it, cut the soil so that you get some of the moss. Look for an interesting, very small piece of wood. It can be a piece of a branch, or a section of bark. Try to find a piece that's soggy, because that means that the process of *decomposition* has already started. As you watch your system begin to work, you can see the wood slowly break down into soil.

If you want to try taking cuttings to root your own plants, cut a 3-inch-long piece off a small plant, and pinch the bottom leaves off. Leave about an inch and a half of bare stem before the leaves start. Put the stem in a small jar of water, and put the jar on a windowsill. Watch for roots to develop on the stem (some plants root this way, and others don't, so don't be discouraged if your first attempt doesn't work). Once the plant has a root system, it is ready to be planted in dirt.

The best soil for your system is potting soil that you buy from a store, because it is light and rich and has had all bacteria removed from it. If anyone in your family grows houseplants, you probably have some potting soil at home. You can also make your own potting soil. Get some soft, loose dirt from outside (if there is a garden at your house, use garden soil). You'll want enough soil so that when the jar is lying on its side, it is about one-third full of dirt. Now add some dead leaves or grass clippings to the dirt (this *organic matter* will combine with the dirt to make a richer and lighter soil). You'll want about the same amount of organic matter as you have dirt.

Next, find some gravel or small rocks. You'll need enough to make a layer about a half-inch thick in the bottom of your jar (remember that the jar will be on its side). You might also want to find an unusual rock to use later on for landscaping.

Bake the soil, the gravel, the rock, and your small piece of wood in the oven, at the lowest setting, for two hours. Be sure to keep the soil and the gravel separate. The baking process (which destroys bacteria) will dry the soil out completely, so you will have to add some water to it before you put it in the jar. Very carefully, scoop the baked soil into a large bowl. Fill a cup with water and slowly sprinkle it, about a fourth of a cup at a time, over the soil. Mix the soil very gently with your hands, adding water until it is damp but not wet. Soak the piece of wood in water until it is wet.

Now you have all the ingredients and are ready to put your system together. Put the jar on its side and spread gravel on the bottom. Put enough of the soil mixture to make a good, solid layer over the gravel or rocks. Now you will probably have to tip the jar up slightly so that when the lid is off, the soil won't fall out. A rolled-up kitchen towel works pretty well for propping it up.

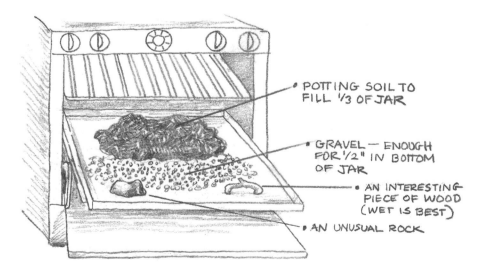

- POTTING SOIL TO FILL ⅓ OF JAR
- GRAVEL — ENOUGH FOR ½" IN BOTTOM OF JAR
- AN INTERESTING PIECE OF WOOD (WET IS BEST)
- AN UNUSUAL ROCK

Once it is propped up, put in more soil until the jar is about one-third full. Now make holes in the dirt to put your plants in, and carefully transplant them into the jar. Don't crowd them — they should be several inches apart. Put your piece of wood in, partially buried, where it looks good (try to make the whole thing look like a miniature landscape). Add your pretty rock. If you can find an earthworm, or even a small cricket or beetle, add it to your system and see what happens.

The best way to water your system is with a spray bottle, but if it is well sealed, and if you start out with enough water in it, you will have to water only rarely, if at all. (Check the system every few weeks to see if the soil feels dry. If it does, spray it with water.) Because it is a closed system, it will recycle its own water.

In the chapters that are coming up, you will find out what makes rain and dew, and you can watch those, and other weather processes, happen in your system-in-a-jar.

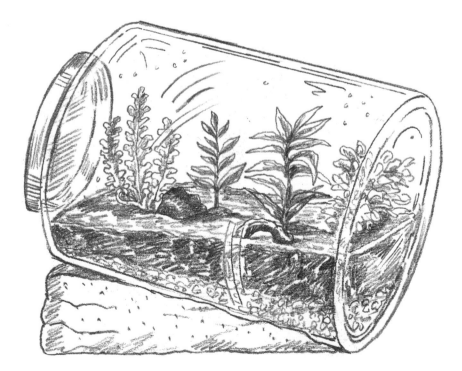

3

The Earthride

Summer, fall, winter, and spring . . . every year we have one of each. You might wish you could skip winter and have spring twice, but it just doesn't happen that way.

Most places on our planet have different weather conditions and day-lengths as one season changes into the next. Since ancient times, people have wanted to know when to expect the rain, the snow, the heat, and the cold, so they have made calendars and other devices to help them predict the seasons. As clever as the ancient people were, though, such devices often disagreed with reality, and the astronomers had to juggle days at the end of each year to make their calendars come out right. It took thousands of years for people to understand the relationship between the sun and the earth, and to figure out what makes day and night, seasons and climates.

Now that we understand it, we can see examples and models of the earth/sun relationship in everyday life. You can find a ride at most amusement parks, for instance, that's called something like "the Octopus." If you can picture our planet circling the sun as if it were on the end of an invisible arm, then this kind of ride is a good model of the relationship between the earth and its sun. Our planet spins like a top at the same time that it circles around the sun at the center of its orbit.

If you've ever been on the Octopus, you know that part of the fun is the fact that your body is going through two different motions at the same time: the seat you're sitting in is spinning around a pole that attaches it to the arm, and then the arm itself is circling around the center. Let's call Earth's trip through space "the Earthride," and we'll take it a few steps further.

Most octopus rides dip up and down as they circle around the center, but the Earthride stays level the whole way around. Most of them have many arms, all the same distance from the center and all moving together. But the eight other arms on the machinery of the Earthride (each one represents one of the other planets in our solar system) all move separately and at different distances from the center. Right now we are concerned with only one of the arms, and that, of course, is the one we're on.

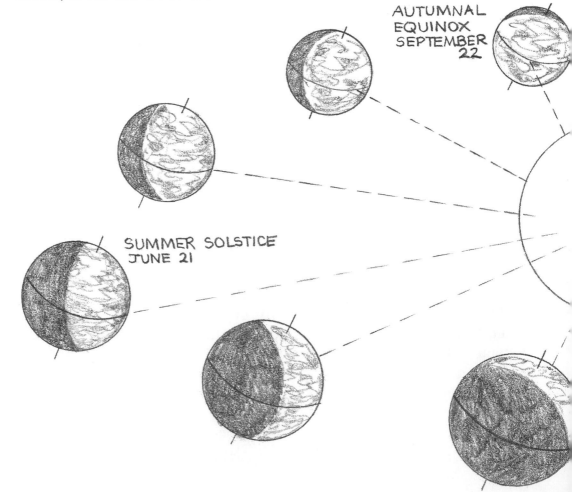

The spinning seats on other octopus rides usually stay level with the arm and dip and climb with the ride. But our planet is attached to the Earthride at a slant, and while the arm stays level all the way around, the planet on the end is always tilted in the same direction. If you understand the tilt of our planet on the Earthride, then you have the key to understanding its seasons.

Not only is the pole that our planet spins around (called the *axis*) attached to the arm at a slant, but no matter where the planet is on its journey around the center of the ride, the axis remains tilted in the same direction. The easiest way to understand that is to look at the picture below. You can see that sometimes the bottom part of the planet is tilting toward the center, and at other times the top part is tilting in.

In the real Earthride, one year is the period of time it takes for the earth to make one complete trip all the way around its sun. When the bottom part of the planet, or the South Pole, is tilted toward the

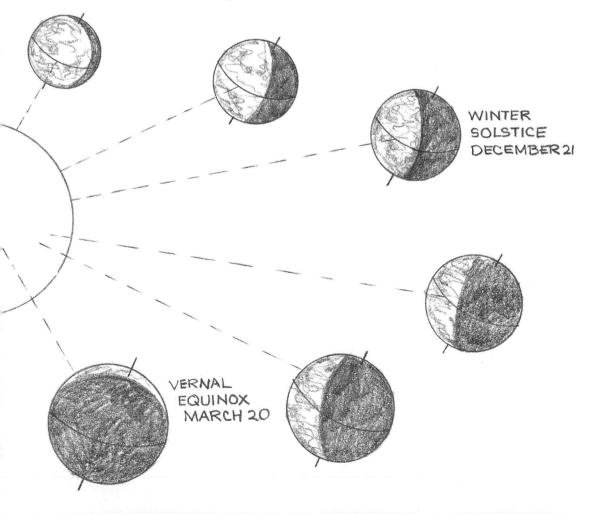

WINTER
SOLSTICE
DECEMBER 21

VERNAL
EQUINOX
MARCH 20

sun, then that part gets more heat and light and is experiencing what we call summer. At the same time that the South Pole is tilted toward the sun, the North Pole is tilted away from it; it is in shadow and is experiencing winter.

Because the hemisphere that is tilted toward the sun gets more light, it also means that days are longer during that time of year. The day that the North Pole is *most* tilted toward the sun is the longest day of the year in the northern hemisphere. The shortest day for that part of the planet, then, is when the South Pole is most tilted toward the sun. These two positions, called the *summer solstice* and *winter solstice*, are at opposite sides of Earth's orbit.

Exactly in between the solstice positions are two places in Earth's orbit where the planet's axis is not tilted toward the sun but is lined up sideways to it (the picture on pages 22 and 23 will help you understand this). At these two times of the year, all parts of the planet get the same amount of light, and days and nights are of equal length everywhere on the globe. These two positions of the Earthride are called the *equinoxes* (the *vernal,* or spring, equinox, and the *autumnal,* or fall, equinox).

The tilt of the earth, then, creates seasons: longer days and warmer weather in the summer, shorter days and colder weather in the winter. Because this is true everywhere on earth, most people on our planet have learned to live with the seasons. As summer changes into autumn, and autumn into winter, many of us dig out a different set of clothes, turn on our heaters, and get ready for colder weather. But for some people, especially those who live and work in the country rather than the city, changes of season mean big changes in their day-to-day lives.

Ranchers and farmers everywhere, for instance, live differently in the summer than they do in the winter. The Navajos, who live in the southwestern part of the United States, balance their lives so that as each season changes, their way of life changes along with it. Here is a story about a Navajo girl.

Jolene Blackgoat is twelve years old. She lives, for most of the year, near the edge of a stark and beautiful canyon in New Mexico. Her family, like many others in the area, moves to a different *hogan* (that means "home for the family") in the spring, in the summer, and again in the winter. The hogans are often very close together — sometimes only a half mile apart — but their different locations provide continuous grazing for the family's sheep.

During the winter Jolene lives at a boarding school in a nearby town, but she returns to her grandparents' hogan as often as possible and is almost always home for the seasonal moves. Jolene's favorite time of the year is the spring. For one thing, that is when her family moves down into the canyon; for another, springtime is when the lambs are born. During the winter the canyon is in shadow most of the time. But in the spring, as the sun climbs higher in the sky, the floor of the canyon warms up and the grass becomes green sooner than up on the rim. So the family moves out of its winter hogan and 600 feet down to the floor of the canyon.

One spring the move down the canyon nearly became a disaster. Jolene was helping her brothers herd the family's sheep down the steep, narrow trail that led to the floor of the canyon when one of the sheep panicked. It crashed into Jolene on the narrow trail and knocked her off the edge.

She bumped and slid for 20 feet, desperately grabbing at bushes and rocks as they flew by, while her brothers scrambled through their herd of frightened sheep trying to get to her. Her fall was finally broken by a tree, but unfortunately her ankle was broken, too. Being carried down the treacherous trail was an experience she tried hard not to remember, but as spring wore on, a kind of balance came back into her life, and she learned to live and be happy with a cast on her leg.

Her broken ankle kept her from doing the things she usually did, so she found herself doing things she usually *didn't.* She had always been taught to get up and greet the sunrise, but she loved to burrow under the covers and sleep as long as possible, and her whole family teased her about being a little potato. Now she looked forward to the dawn, and as she watched the sun rise, day after day, she saw things that she had never noticed before.

For instance, when her family planted their corn in the canyon, the sun was coming up between two standing rocks up on the rim. But on the day that the first plants sprouted, the sun came up behind one of the rocks instead of between them, and each day it rose just a little farther toward the north. (Of course the sun always rose in the east and set in the west, but as the earth moved into the summer solstice position, the sun seemed to move toward the north.) Each day was also getting a little longer, and she realized that she was waking up just a tiny bit earlier to greet the dawn.

The lambs were born, the corn got taller, and the sun kept rising farther to the north. One day her grandfather said it was time to move up to the summer hogan: the lambs were old enough for the journey, and most of the grass had been grazed off the floor of the canyon. The summer hogan was up on the mountain, where there was a corral for the sheep and a well for water. This time Jolene rode the long way around in her grandfather's truck, and her brothers took the sheep and horses up the canyon trail.

It was a little bit cooler up on the mountain, but still the summer was very hot. The sun was higher in the sky each day, and the days themselves were still getting longer. Jolene's father told her that the day the sun got highest in the sky and rose farthest toward the north would be the longest day of the year, and then the sun would start its journey back to the south. She was beginning to understand why that happened, and she could clearly see the results of it in her own life and in the lives of all living things around her.

The longest day of the year came, and Jolene marked it by noticing exactly where on the horizon the sun rose and set. She knew that she would now watch the sun on its journey to the south, and that on the day when it rose farthest toward the south it would be winter, and she would be living at the school in Crownpoint. That would be the shortest day of the year — the winter solstice in December — and when she came home for Christmas, her family would be living in their winter hogan on the rim of the canyon.

Jolene knew something about the journey of the sun and the seasons that she hadn't known before, and she also knew that she would never lose that knowledge. It would become part of her own relationship with the earth and would help her to understand the ways of her people.

The more we notice and understand about the world around us, by watching the sun's journey and the march of the seasons, or by noticing weather changes and the things that signal them, the quicker our journey toward weatherwisdom will be. In the next chapter we'll find out about what makes climates, but first, here are some fun things to do that will help you understand the Earthride and the seasons.

The Planet Game

For this game you need a dark room, at least two people, a flashlight, an orange or apple, and a pencil. First, you have to turn the orange or apple into a model of the earth: the top of the fruit, where the stem is, is the North Pole, and the bottom is the South Pole. Push the pencil through the fruit so that the eraser end sticks out of the North Pole and the sharp end sticks out of the South Pole. The pencil represents the axis of the planet.

Now, the person who is "it" stands with the flashlight in the middle of the dark room. She is the sun. The other person will carry the earth on its journey around the sun. The person who is the sun will turn very slowly so that the light is always shining on the planet.

THE SUN →

SLOWLY TURNING

Meanwhile, the one who is carrying the earth in its orbit has to make sure that the pencil is always held at the same angle and pointing in the same direction. For instance, when he starts walking, the eraser end of the pencil might be pointing to a particular wall. As he slowly circles around the sun, he has to make sure that the eraser end of the pencil is always pointing toward the same wall. The game won't work unless the planet always remains tilted in the same direction.

The light from the flashlight makes daylight and darkness on the piece of fruit just as the sun does on the earth. When the sharpened end of the pencil, or the South Pole, is tilted toward the sun, it is summer in the southern hemisphere and winter in the northern. When the eraser end of the pencil, or the North Pole, is tilted toward the sun, summer and winter are reversed. You will see that these two solstice positions are on opposite sides of the circle that the planet makes around the sun.

The equinoxes happen when the pencil is neither pointing toward nor away from the sun, but is lined up sideways to it. When this happens, it is either spring or fall, depending on which hemisphere you're talking about.

Here is how the game works: the person who is walking the earth around its orbit stops at random, and the one who is "it" has to say what season is happening in either the northern or southern hemisphere at that point in the orbit (for example, "winter in the northern hemisphere," or "spring in the southern hemisphere"). Spring and fall are the trickiest because they look the same. The only way to tell is to figure out whether the hemisphere in question is in between summer and winter (which would make it fall), or in between winter and summer (which would make it spring).

Every correct answer is one point, but if the person who is "it" misses, she loses her turn and trades places with the one who is carrying the planet. Keep score, and the person with the most points wins. If you disagree about whether someone is right or wrong, use the picture on pages 22 and 23 to help you figure it out.

Stonehenge Revisited

The standing stones of Stonehenge, in England, show how ancient cultures built huge instruments to help them measure time and seasons. You can build a smaller version in your own backyard. All you need is some sticks and stones and a flat place that gets direct sunlight.

First, find a straight stick that's about a foot and a half long, and bury one end 6 inches or so in the ground so that the top is sticking straight up. Part of this instrument is a compass, so first you have to find and mark the four directions. To do this, put a pebble at the end of the stick's shadow when you get up in the morning, and measure the length of the shadow. In the afternoon, when the shadow is the same length as the morning shadow, put another pebble at the end of the new shadow. If you put the tip of your left foot on the first pebble, and of your right foot on the second, your body will be facing north.

MORNING SHADOW

AFTERNOON SHADOW

Put a stone to mark north about a foot in front of the stick, and then use a string or a yardstick to make a straight line from the north stone, through where the standing stick is, to a point about a foot behind it. Place another stone there to mark south. Then, to find east and west, use your string or yardstick to make another line that forms a cross with the north–south line. Put stones about a foot from the stick on either side of it, and they will be east and west.

Now, at the same time every day, either sunrise, noon, or sunset, put a pebble on the end of the shadow of the stick. (At sunrise or sunset you may have trouble finding the shadow's end, so put the pebble on the shadow a little less than a foot from the standing stick.) If you mark the shadow at noon, you will end up marking the solstices; if you use the sunrise or sunset shadow, you'll be marking the equinoxes.

Here's how it works. On the day the noon shadow is longest, that's the winter solstice; when it's shortest, it is the summer solstice. On the day the sunset shadow is due east — or the sunrise is due west — that is either the spring or the autumn equinox. But unless you live in a very flat landscape, where you can see the sun rise or set on a distant horizon, the equinoxes may be off by a day or two. Use either sticks or tall stones to mark any of these positions; they will be the same, year after year.

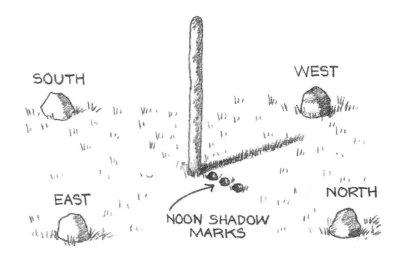

SOUTH

WEST

EAST

NORTH

NOON SHADOW
MARKS

4

What Makes Climates?

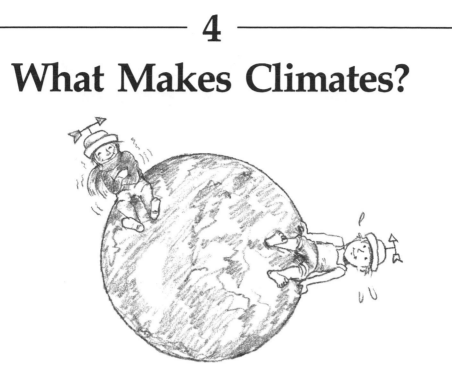

If you live in Mexico City, you probably won't have a white Christmas, and if you live in Barrow, Alaska, you won't swelter on the Fourth of July. Different parts of our planet have very different climates and, of course, very different weather, too.

We learned in Chapter 2 that our planet works like one huge system, using the atmosphere to distribute the sun's energy (called *solar radiation*) to all parts of its surface. And we learned in Chapter 3 that because of the way the Earthride is set up, some parts of the planet receive much more solar radiation than others. If we combine what we learned in those two chapters, then we can begin to understand why climates happen where they do.

We know, for instance, that a band around the middle of the earth, reaching a little way above and below the equator, gets more heat and light all year round than any other part of the globe. In other words, there is a surplus of solar energy at the equator (a surplus is an amount of something that exists over and above what is needed). Even when one pole or the other is tilted away from the sun, the middle part of the earth is always facing into it, so the surplus at the equator is a permanent condition.

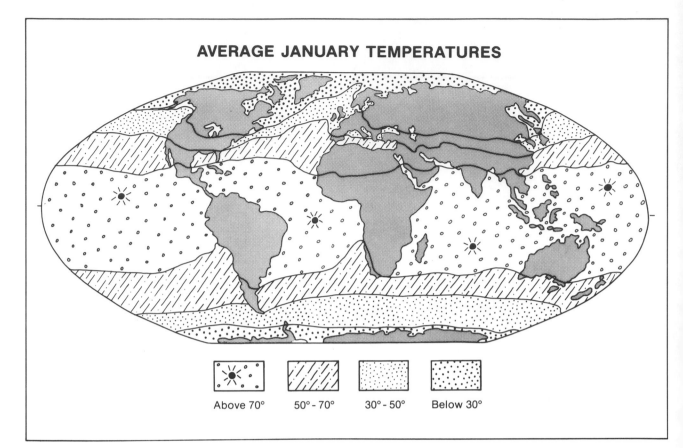

AVERAGE JANUARY TEMPERATURES

| Above 70° | 50° - 70° | 30° - 50° | Below 30° |

Since one of the jobs of a system is to maintain a balance between all of its parts, the system called Earth is continually moving heat energy from the equator to the poles. The way it does that is to use the circulation of air in the atmosphere (and water in the oceans) to carry heat from places that are too hot to places that are too cold. This mechanism is called *global circulation,* and it helps to account for climates.

If you put something into circulation, you are making it move. Air that is moving is called wind. A very long time ago, people thought that wind was created by angels flapping their wings. But people began to realize that wind is something that happens naturally because of the heating of our planet by the sun, and because of its rotation around the sun. Here is how it works:

One of the basic laws of global circulation is that warm air rises and cold air sinks. Air that is warmed near the equator rises and begins to move toward the poles. As it reaches the upper atmosphere, it cools off again and sinks back toward the earth. Because air has weight, just like anything else, an interesting thing happens when it lifts and then sinks down again.

As the warm air at the equator rises, it creates a belt of *low pressure* all around the middle of the planet, where the weight of the air has been lifted. (This belt is called the *equatorial trough.*) When that air cools and sinks back down at a different place, it creates a zone of *high pressure,* where the weight of the air is pressing down. Well, guess what happens? Air flows exactly like water: from high to low areas. So if there is a low-pressure zone, air will flow into it just as if it were a low place in your yard that fills up with water after a rain. Movement of air from areas of high pressure to areas of low pressure creates wind.

If our planet weren't spinning on its axis, this air-in-motion, or wind, would rise and move away from the equator toward either of the poles, and then, after it cooled and sank, it would move back toward the low-pressure zone around the equator. Either way, it would be moving in a northerly or southerly direction. Since the earth is spinning, though, the wind flowing back toward the equator is turned to the side, or *deflected,* by the spinning of the earth.

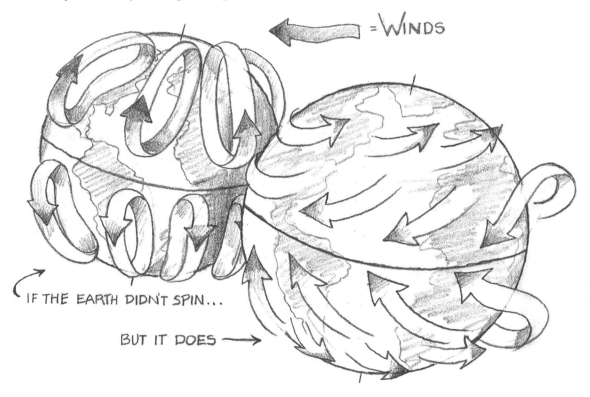

= WINDS

IF THE EARTH DIDN'T SPIN...

BUT IT DOES →

Both flowing air and flowing water are deflected in one direction in the northern hemisphere and in the opposite direction in the southern hemisphere. Here is an interesting fact: water flows into the drains of sinks and bathtubs (and usually toilets) in a counterclockwise direction in the northern hemisphere, and in a clockwise direction in the southern hemisphere. You can fill, then empty, your sink and check it out. Air follows the same general pattern: when it is moving into a low-pressure system in the northern hemisphere, it is almost always set into a counterclockwise spin.

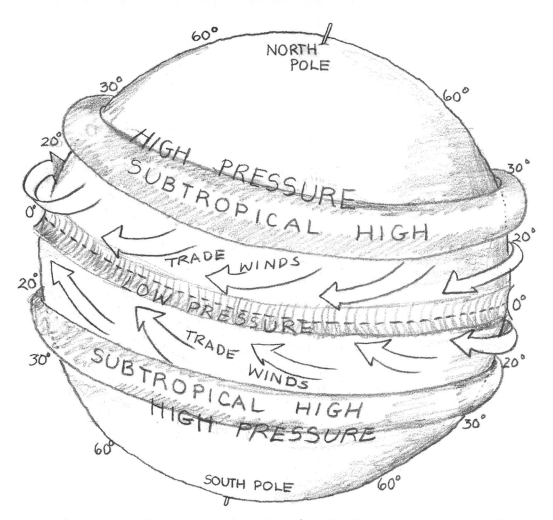

So now we know that there is a band of low pressure encircling the earth near the equator, where air that has been warmed by the sun lifts into the atmosphere. There are also belts of high pressure north and south of the equator, where that same air has cooled and sunk back to the surface of the planet. These belts are called the *subtropical highs,* and they are centered between 20° and 30° north and south of the equator. The fact that such high- and low-pressure zones exist, and that they shift north and south with the seasons, is part of what makes global climates.

For one thing, these major areas of high and low pressure cause winds that occur all over the globe. For instance, because of the way the planet is spinning, air that is moving into the equatorial trough from both the north and south is bent toward the west. So there are two steady bands of wind blowing all the way around the globe from east to west, just above and below the equator. These winds are called the *trade winds.*

The trade winds are so reliable that sailors and navigators have used them for hundreds of years to move across the ocean in a westerly direction. Christopher Columbus, knowing that Portuguese ships coasted westward off the coast of Africa on a reliable wind, guessed that if he sailed his ships into that wind it would take them all the way to China. Well, he was right about the wind, but wrong about China, because there was another landmass in the way. As we now know, he ended up discovering the New World instead of finding the court of the Great Khan.

When he gave up on China and headed for home, Columbus sailed north, hoping to find a wind that would blow him back to the east. Once again his guess was correct, and after sailing two weeks to the northeast, he found the winds that are now called the *westerlies*. The westerlies blow from west to east in both the southern and the northern hemispheres, in two broad bands around the planet that are called the *midlatitude zones.*

All over the world, then, climates are affected by winds that blow hot or cold, wet or dry, and by the high- and low-pressure areas that create them. If you live where the trade winds converge, for instance, you are in a climate that's hot all year round (being close to the equator), and usually wet because the trade winds pick up moisture from the oceans and drop it on the land as they pass over. (In the next chapter we'll find out about a girl who lives in a wet equatorial climate.)

If you live around 30° north or south latitude, you might be in one of the world's greatest deserts. Areas that are beneath these two high-pressure belts often have desert climates, because air that is returning to the surface of the earth from the upper atmosphere has lost most of its moisture. (There is a story in the next chapter about a boy who lives in the desert.)

A little bit farther away from the equator in either direction are the midlatitude zones, from about 35° to about 55°, where the prevailing westerlies blow. There are many types of climates that occur in the midlatitudes (and because most of the United States is in this zone of latitude, you probably live in one of them), but they all have a few things in common. For one thing, they are far enough away from the equator to experience a change of seasons as their part of the earth is

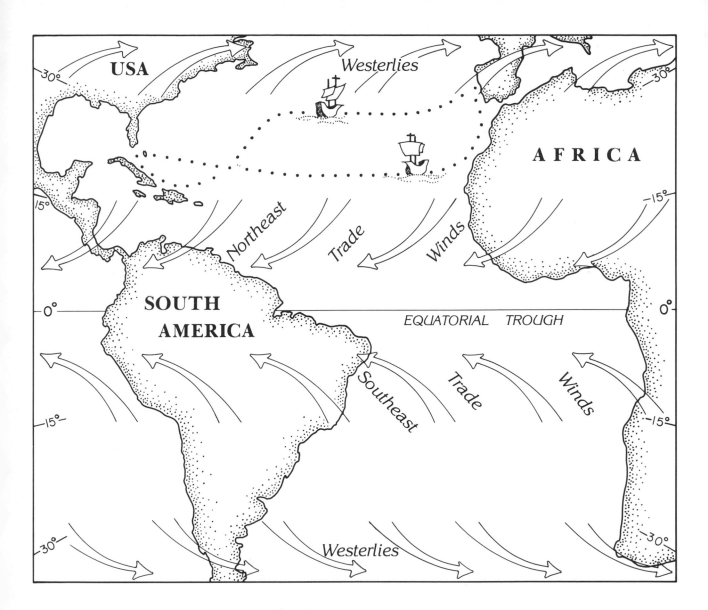

tilted either toward or away from the sun. (Jolene Blackgoat, whom we met in Chapter 3, lives in a midlatitude climate.)

Another thing that happens in the midlatitudes is that cold air from the poles meets warm air from the tropics and creates all sorts of weather disturbances. When air masses that are very different in temperature or moisture content run into each other, they collide and cause major weather events. If you've ever heard about *cold fronts* or *warm fronts*, then you already know something about these collisions. Fronts hold some of the secrets for predicting weather, and we'll find out more about them in Chapter 7.

You can easily guess what *high-latitude* (polar, or arctic and antarctic) climates are like. The first thing that comes to mind, of course, is cold: finger-numbing, teeth-chattering, freezing cold. We know that the reason high latitudes are cold is the way our planet tilts as it orbits around the sun in the Earthride.

Because of that tilt, there are many months of the year when one pole or the other is pointing away from the sun. Near the poles, in the high latitudes, there is no direct sunshine and so no direct warming of the land or oceans during the winter months. Even though there are also many months when one pole or the other is pointing toward the sun, solar radiation strikes the land at such a low angle that it doesn't provide much heat. These areas depend on circulation of air or water from warmer parts of the planet for almost all the heat they get.

Another thing that happens in high latitudes is that, during winter months, the land masses are under huge high-pressure areas, similar to the belts of high pressure between 20° and 30° north and south of the equator. The same thing happens in the polar regions as in the sub-tropics: the high-pressure areas create desertlike conditions on the land underneath. The presence of snow and ice in artic and antarctic regions can fool you: it is there because it rarely melts, not because of frequent snowstorms.

We have learned a little about global circulation and about low-, mid-, and high-latitude climates. In the next chapter we'll find out about children who live in some of these climates. But first, here's another instrument to add to your weather station.

—————— Weather Station II ——————

Evangelista Toriccelli, the first man to measure the weight of the atmosphere, called it an "ocean of air." He had to fight the popular opinion of his time (around 1640) to prove that air, like water, has weight. But, as we now know, it is the weight of the atmosphere (or its pressure) that causes wind and the movement of air throughout the system. Luckily for us, Toriccelli believed in his own ideas (and those of his teacher, Galileo) and, as a result, invented the world's first instrument for measuring the weight of the atmosphere.

His instrument, now called a *barometer,* provided a way to study how changes in *atmospheric pressure* are related to weather. If you can measure and record the atmospheric pressure yourself, you will discover definite patterns in your weather record. You'll learn that low pressure brings one kind of weather and that high pressure brings another. Since Toriccelli's invention is so useful, the next instrument you will make for your weather station is a barometer.

BAROMETER. To make this instrument you will need a small drinking glass with straight sides, a ruler, some strong tape, about one foot of clear plastic tubing (you can buy it in a hardware or hobby store), and a piece of chewing gum. First, tape the ruler to the glass so that it doesn't move (use tape at the bottom and top of the glass). Now put the plastic tube in the glass so that the end of the tube is about half an inch from the bottom of the glass, and tape it to the ruler in two places so that it won't move, either.

This is the fun part: Chew the piece of gum so that it's nice and gooey, and then leave it in the side of your mouth for a minute. Now fill the glass about halfway with water, and then use the tube as if it were a straw and suck water into the tube until it's about half full. With the tube still in your mouth, use your tongue to quickly seal the end of the tube with gum so that the water doesn't flow back out of it. By sealing the top of the tube, you have created a vacuum above the level of the water.

Because air has weight, it is constantly pushing down on everything on earth. When atmospheric pressure is high, there is more weight pushing down on things, and when it is low, there is less. The weight of air pushing down on the water in the glass will force the column of water in the tube to move up when the pressure is high, or to move down when it is low.

You will need some sort of pen or marker to make a scale on the ruler. If you mark the level of water in the tube every day, you will end up with a series of lines that move a short distance up and down the ruler. Without knowing exactly what each of those lines means, you can still tell whether the pressure is high, normal, or low, and whether it is rising or falling. Since the barometer is affected by changing temperature, it is best to keep it inside your house, where the temperature is more steady. Now you can add the barometric pressure to your daily weather record.

5

From the Jungle to the Desert

Our planet has a fantastic selection of climates to offer any Earthling who has a taste for variety. Some of them are mild, and some are very harsh. But no matter what they're like, there are probably people living in them. From the arctic tundra, where 200-year-old trees are just 4 inches high and people live in houses made of ice, to equatorial rain forests, where life is so exuberant that trees are almost as tall as skyscrapers and spiders are the size of dinner plates, human beings have learned to adapt to the climate they live in.

The island of Borneo lies right on the equator. Its location means that it gets two and a half times as much solar radiation as the poles, but atmospheric circulation carries away 80 percent of the surplus energy and keeps the island from overheating. There is more than enough rainfall to keep rivers full throughout the year and to water hundreds of thousands of acres of jungle. Borneo is the third largest island in the world, and it is almost entirely covered with equatorial rain forest.

The inside of a rain forest is one of the strangest and most beautiful environments in the world. The sky there is almost entirely closed out by a green roof, far overhead, where the top branches of huge trees meet to form a canopy that goes for miles in every direction.

Although sunlight enters through the green canopy, by the time it reaches the ground, it has been filtered through millions of leaves and is a soft greenish-gold color. Orchids and vines hang down from high branches, and every once in a while a shaft of sunlight enters through a hole in the roof of leaves. Tiny plants grow on small plants, and small plants grow on big plants; trunks and branches of trees are shaggy with ferns and mosses, and even boulders in the river are covered with soft green fur.

This is Abat's home, and although she has never lived in any one place longer than a few months, she has also never left the rain forest. She is about eleven years old, but doesn't know for sure because her people don't keep track of the years. Since Borneo is at the equator, there are no distinct seasons to help mark the passage of time, and clues from the moon and stars are invisible under the roof of the rain forest.

Abat's people are the Penan. Because they spend all their lives outside, they have adapted their culture almost perfectly to the equatorial climate. Instead of building permanent villages, they live for a few weeks or months wherever they find a large stand of sago palms. There they make sago flour and hunt for wild pigs.

The shelters that Abat's people make are perfect for the rain-forest climate and blend into the jungle so well that they're practically invisible. They are built in an hour or less, using only materials found in the forest. The roofs are made of three layers of fan-palm leaves to provide protection from the rains that fall almost every night, and the platforms are made of saplings lashed together with rattan. They are built several feet off the ground, both to allow air to circulate underneath, and to keep leeches, snakes, and fire ants from inviting themselves to dinner.

The jungle provides almost all that the people need, but it also holds many dangers. One day Abat and her cousin, Jangang, encountered one of them. They had gone down to the river to make sago flour, and after working hard for many hours had bathed and rinsed their clothes in the river. They were playing on a log and Jangang was pretending to be a hunter when he suddenly yelped and jumped into the air.

At first Abat thought it was part of his game, but she had seen something flash along the ground away from the log and soon realized he had been bitten by a snake. Life and death come quickly in the jungle, but Abat knew if she was fast she could save Jangang's life. She had seen a vine called *tawan-turok* growing nearby. She ran back to that place, cut a piece of vine, and then returned to Jangang, who was lying on the ground next to the log.

Abat used the handle of her knife to pound the vine into a gooey pulp, and then spread it over the wound on her cousin's ankle. By the time Abat had gone for help to carry Jangang back to camp, he seemed to be in less pain. The next day, Abat knew that her cousin would survive the snakebite. Her people had lived for hundreds of years in the rain forest and had figured out how to turn the hot, humid climate and lush vegetation to their advantage. Like all children, she learned from the people around her the lessons they learned in their own childhood.

Our environments teach us how to live in them: if it is cold, we build ingenious shelters and make warm clothing; if it is hot, our shelters are just as clever, but they serve a different purpose; if it is dry, we learn to conserve water and do without it. Human beings seem to be able to adapt to most environments. The Tuareg of the Sahara, for instance, live in the greatest desert on our planet.

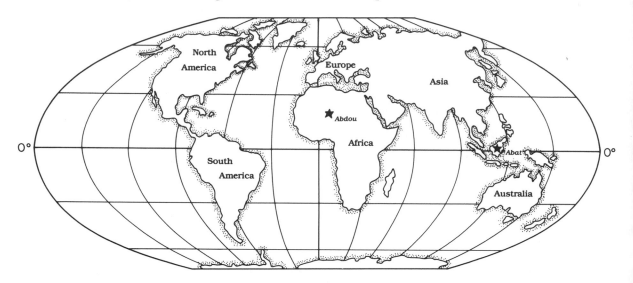

The Sahara is really made up of several deserts stretched out next to each other in the northern third of Africa. Together they cover nearly as much area as the United States (minus Alaska). Rain is so rare in the Sahara that parts of the desert go for many years without getting a single drop. It is only the presence of rivers running underground beneath the sand that makes life in the desert possible. Every once in a while the underground rivers come up to the surface, where they form pools or even long, winding lakes, and these places are called *oases*.

An oasis in the middle of the desert is an amazing sight. Everything else as far as the eye can see is white and parched and shimmering with heat. But even from a distance, an oasis is a cool, sparkling green. It looks as if all of the palm trees that wanted to grow in the desert for thousands of miles around have crowded into the small space of the oasis. And not just the palm trees, but other plants, animals, and people, too. Outside of the oases, there are few creatures of any kind that can survive.

For hundreds of years the Tuareg were the lords of the desert, not just because they had found a way to live there, but because they controlled the caravan routes, which meant all the transportation, across the three million square miles of the Sahara. Now that there are jeeps and trucks that cross the desert more easily than camels, the Tuareg way of life is disappearing. Most of the Tuareg have settled in oasis villages, but it is still possible to find their camps in the isolated mountains of the Central Desert.

Abdou is a twelve-year-old *Tarqi* (the word *Tarqi* means one single Tuareg) who lives in the Ahaggar region of the Sahara. (You can see where that is on the map on page 46.) His family raises camels and goats, both for themselves and for their kinspeople who live in a nearby town. The mountains of Ahaggar would look to most of us like a picture of the moon, and it is hard to imagine how anyone could survive there. Although Ahaggar isn't in the region of the great sand dunes, there is drifting sand everywhere between the rocks and boulders of the mountains.

Ahaggar is under one of the belts of high pressure that run around the earth about 30° north and south of the equator. Normally there is little movement of the hot, dry air, but when a low-pressure system develops over the Mediterranean Sea (about 900 miles to the north), the hot desert air is sucked into the "low" at tremendous speeds, creating the dreaded sirocco wind. The sirocco blows only rarely, but even when the air is still, it is hot and dry, and only people who have adapted to desert conditions can live there.

Abdou's world is brown. Very few plants can survive in the mountains of Ahaggar, and the rare scrubby bushes that do grow seem to produce more thorns than leaves. So, unlike the mountain home of Abat on Borneo, the desert has no green. There are no plants for people to eat (since we don't have mouths like camels or goats, who can eat thorns), or to make houses, tools, and medicines out of. The only water to be found in the mountains is in the natural rock water holes, which are very important to the Tuareg.

One day Abdou's mother asked him to take two of the family's camels to the nearest *guelta,* or water hole, and bring back water for the camp. He packed enough food for a two-day trip, put a saddle on one camel and loaded the other with empty water bags, and rode out of camp in the morning.

Early in the afternoon Abdou noticed that the light on the horizon was a strange yellow color and that the air was so full of electricity that when he touched his water bag, sparks flew from his fingers, making little popping sounds. He knew this meant the sirocco was coming and that there would soon be a terrible sandstorm. Within a few minutes his camels knew, too, and they started bellowing and shrieking as only camels can.

Abdou looked around for shelter, knowing that he had only minutes in which to find protection for himself and his animals. The best he could hope for would be a space between two rocky outcrops, and even there they could be buried by flying sand. His search for shelter was almost frantic, and he blessed his good fortune when he found a place where he could hide from the furious storm. Abdou soon persuaded his panic-stricken camels into the narrow space, and they all knelt down to wait for the wind to die.

During the sandstorm Abdou was glad of the protection of his veil, wrapped around his head with only a narrow slit for his eyes. When he put his head down and pulled his robes tight, he was somewhat protected from the storm, but the camels continued to shriek in fear and pain as they were whipped with flying particles of sand. It seemed as though the storm lasted forever, and all Abdou could think of was water. It felt as if every drop of liquid was being sucked from his body.

When the storm finally passed, Abdou had to dig himself and the camels out of the sand. He allowed himself a small drink from his almost-empty water bag, and then continued on his way to the *guelta*. Even with the delay of the storm, he got there by nightfall. He camped by the water hole that night and returned home, loaded with water, the next day. His family was very relieved to see him, but they had known that his skill in the desert could be trusted to get him through the sirocco.

Abdou's weatherwisdom, his knowledge of the desert, his clothing, food, shelter, and animals — all show how his people have adapted to their harsh climate. Abdou's people, the Tuareg, and Abat's people, the Penan, are examples of how we humans have learned to live in the various climates of our world. Whether you realize it or not, you are well adapted to your own climate. Although in our culture we rarely have to create emergency protection for ourselves, it's nice to think that we could if we had to. Would you like to find out how inventive you are? Here's an activity that will test your skills.

Can You Adapt?

What kind of homemade weather protection do you think you can make or build for yourself? There are two basic kinds of protection you can experiment with: protection for your body itself, such as clothing, and protection from the weather, as in shelters outside (in the woods, on the sand, in the dirt or snow, and so on).

Here are some basic rules:

1. If you are making body protection, don't wreck anyone else's property. You can use things like plastic garbage bags (as long as you cut a neck hole and keep your head out of it), unused cardboard boxes, and so on.

2. Don't destroy anything in the environment. You can build a snow cave, a lean-to in the woods with deadwood or fallen branches, shade at the beach out of driftwood and clothing, and so on. But you can't cut down trees or pull branches off them.

6

The Weather Machine

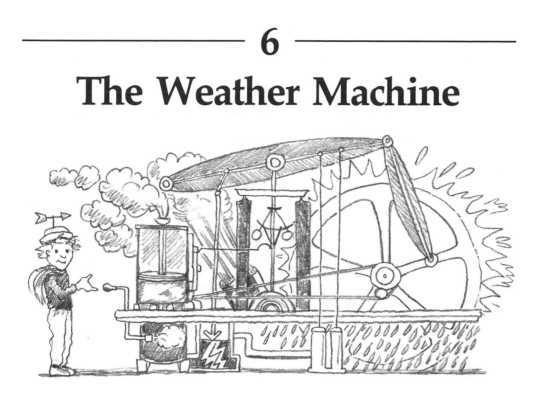

If you think of the word *energy,* what comes to mind? Power? Force? Strength? Although we each might use the word in a slightly different way, we probably have a good idea that without energy, nothing much would happen. The fact is that, no matter how you define it, energy is what makes any kind of movement or change possible.

In this book we've talked about energy in three main ways: it comes from the sun; it's the fuel for just about all activity on Earth; and our system carries it from place to place to keep the world from boiling over or freezing solid. Now we'll find out exactly how weather distributes energy over the surface of our planet.

We know that the sun is Earth's powerhouse and that our planet intercepts only a minute fraction of the sun's total output. But even that tiny fraction (one-half of one-billionth of the total) is a huge amount. We get as much energy each minute from the sun as the total amount of electricity generated in one year by all the power plants on earth.

You can imagine that if our planet absorbed all that energy, it would soon look like a cinder. But the earth doesn't just absorb solar energy, it uses it first, and then recycles it back out into space. All of the energy we receive from the sun is eventually returned to space, so our system is constantly working to maintain a balance. The atmosphere, our "ocean of air," is the key to that balance.

Some kinds of solar energy (like ultraviolet radiation, which is harmful to living organisms) are mostly filtered out by the topmost layers of our atmosphere and never reach the ground. Then, of the solar radiation that penetrates through the upper atmosphere, a certain amount of it is scattered or reflected back into space by clouds or by the ground (you'll learn how that works if you play Merc's Albedo game at the end of this chapter).

The rest of the energy that enters our atmosphere is absorbed either by atmospheric gases and clouds or by the ground. This is the energy that ends up being used by the system to provide heat, light, and other useful forms of radiation to the planet. After it circulates through the system, this energy, too, is returned to space.

But what happens to solar energy while it's still in our atmosphere? If weather is the way the sun's energy gets distributed over the surface of our planet, then weather processes must involve converting energy into a form that, first of all, can be stored, then transported from one place to another, and, finally, released at some new destination. Here is an example of how a system that you're very familiar with might do that:

Say you eat a Nutri-blast Health Bar. The system that is your body converts it into fuel. It stores most of the fuel, using just a small amount to transport itself to the beach. At the beach, the energy that your body converted, stored, and transported there gets used for normal beach activities, such as swimming, volleyball, chasing a Frisbee — and perhaps grabbing a bucket, filling it with water, and dumping it on an unsuspecting friend who is lying on the sand reading a book!

Both the system called Earth and the system that is your body process energy by converting it to a usable form, storing it so that it can be transported, and moving it to where it is going to be released. The system called Earth uses the atmosphere and weather to accomplish all this, and, strangely enough, water is the key to how it works.

Whenever water changes form (it can be a solid, a liquid, or a gas), the conversion uses or releases a lot of energy. With the input of energy from the sun, water is converted from one form to another, and in the process, energy is stored and transported through the atmosphere.

No matter where you live, you are probably familiar with the conversion of water into its different forms. If you drop an ice cube onto the floor, you soon have a messy puddle. If your parents don't put antifreeze in the car's radiator, the water in it may freeze and cause unhealthy cracks in the engine block. When you take a shower, the bathroom is full of moisture that collects on the mirror and makes it impossible to see your reflection.

LEMONADE ADDS HEAT TO ICE

All of these transformations either use or release energy. You know that in order to change water from a solid (ice) into a liquid, something must be added — and that something is energy in the form of heat. So when you put a few ice cubes into a glass of lemonade, heat is removed from the lemonade and added to the ice in the process of changing the ice into water. And if you drink it right after the ice melts, you end up with very cold but slightly watery lemonade.

What if you decided to make a lemon popsicle out of the rest of your lemonade? It would take exactly the same amount of energy to turn the water in the lemonade back into ice as it did to turn the ice cubes into water (only this time heat energy would be removed from the water instead of added to it).

Even more energy is used in the process of changing water from a liquid into a gas, called *vapor*. In order for *evaporation* to happen, heat energy must be added to the water and removed from the air around it to change the water from a liquid to a gas. That means that evaporation is a cooling process. You've experienced this cooling process first hand thousands of times. Did you ever notice that the air always feels cooler when you're wet? That's because heat is being taken from the air right around your body to evaporate the water on your skin.

The heat energy that is used when water is changed from liquid into vapor is stored right in the vapor itself. Then, when it is turned from vapor back into water (a process called *condensation*), that same amount of energy is released. Anytime you see a cloud in the sky, you are looking at a powerhouse of energy that was released when water vapor condensed into the microscopically small droplets that form a cloud. The energy that is given off when water vapor turns into raindrops is what hurricanes and tornadoes use as fuel.

Have you ever noticed that when you take a shower on a hot day, the bathroom mirror doesn't cloud up as much as it does on a cold day? That's because warm air can hold a lot more moisture than cold air can, and it isn't until air is cooled to a certain point (called its *dew point*) that condensation happens and the vapor in the air is turned back into water.

A perfect example of this process is the way water condenses on the outside of a cold glass of liquid. This happens because the air right around the outside of the glass is much colder than the surrounding air (in fact it has been cooled to its dew point), so the water vapor in the air condenses and forms droplets on the outside of the glass.

Whoever designed car defrosters understood the relationship between temperature and condensation, and realized that if you heat the air next to the windshield on the inside of the car, it will become warmer and will hold the moisture in it as vapor instead of condensing it into water droplets.

(You can experiment with the condensation process by cooling the air in your system-in-a-jar and watching water droplets form on the inside of the glass. If the drops get big enough, it will rain in your jar. The best way to cool the jar is to put it in a cold place — in the refrigerator, if there's enough room, or right in front of an air conditioner. Don't let the temperature drop below freezing, though, or the plants will die.)

You can see, then, that water in any of its forms is one of the most important components of weather. Not only is water important for its own sake, but it is also the way energy gets transported around the system. The cycle that water goes through as it changes from one form to another and travels from the earth's surface up into the atmosphere and then back down to the ground again is called the *hydrologic cycle*. Since this is such an important part of understanding weather, let's make up a water molecule named Molly and go through the whole cycle with her.

To begin with, Molly the Molecule is drifting on the surface of the Pacific Ocean, about 20° north of the equator. The sun has been beating down on the water for several hours, and by about 2 o'clock in the afternoon, the surface of the ocean has absorbed enough heat energy to break Molly away from the water she is swimming in. Suddenly she is sucked up into the sky by evaporation and becomes part of a parcel of air that is floating upward like a hot-air balloon.

She has plenty of company in her parcel of air because millions of other molecules were evaporated at the same time she was. They all drift slowly upward until their parcel cools to the same temperature as the air around it, and by that time they are a few miles above the surface of the ocean. Because the parcel of air has been cooled to its

The Adventures of Molly

dew point, all of the water molecules in it condense into microscopically tiny water droplets. Molly and the other molecules have become part of a cloud. (That's quite a trick — they used to be part of an ocean, then they were an invisible part of the air, now they are part of a cloud, and in a week or two they're going to be part of some raindrops.)

As Molly's cloud drifts toward the Hawaiian Islands, it gets caught in the circulation of air around a high-pressure system and is spun off to the north and east. In just over a week and a half, Molly and the other molecules have traveled from Hawaii to Minnesota, and now weather conditions are right for turning the tiny droplets of water in her cloud into rain.

It takes 15 million cloud droplets to form one drop of rain, so somehow Molly and the other molecules have to get fastened together into a raindrop. Here is how it happens: Because their cloud is a few miles above the ground, the temperature in it is below freezing. For some reason, ice attracts water vapor, so in a cloud like Molly's, if ice crystals are close to water droplets, water molecules will evaporate from the droplets and condense onto the ice crystals.

That is just what happens to Molly. She becomes part of a droplet that forms around an ice crystal, and as it falls toward the ground, it picks up more water droplets and becomes heavier and heavier. Falling

the Molecule

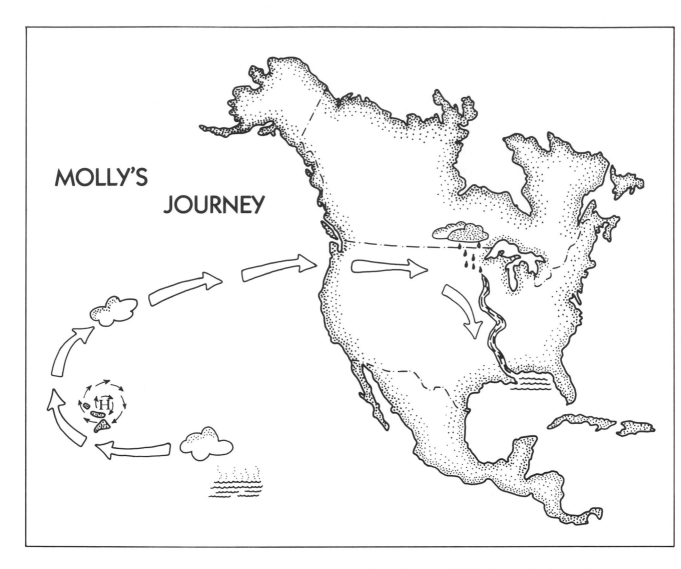

MOLLY'S JOURNEY

through warmer air, the ice crystal melts, and Molly and the others finally become part of a raindrop.

When Molly's raindrop reaches the ground, it lands first on the leaf of a tree, and then it drips onto a rock that is at the edge of a small stream. When her drop runs into the stream, Molly is back in the water again. Her little stream flows into the great Mississippi River, and after many weeks of traveling, Molly eventually gets back to the ocean (only this time it happens to be the Gulf of Mexico).

The hydrologic cycle has kept water on our planet recycling for billions of years, and through it our atmosphere delivers water to us in the form of precipitation (rain, snow, sleet, hail, and so on). But precipitation is one of the last steps in the cycle. Before it can happen, water must go through all the other steps.

You know that condensation occurs automatically whenever a parcel of air is cooled below its dew point. That's why Molly and the other molecules became a cloud when their parcel of air lifted into the sky and cooled. They changed from invisible water vapor into microscopically tiny droplets that formed a white, fluffy cloud.

But as you may have noticed, not every cloud makes precipitation. Learning how to tell the difference between a cloud that will probably make rain (or some other form of precipitation) and one that won't is a very important part of weatherwisdom. In the next chapter we'll find out about storm systems — what they look like and how they deliver precipitation to the surface of the earth. But first, here is a game to help you understand how solar radiation is reflected and absorbed.

—————— Merc's Albedo Game ——————

One day a friend of mine was sitting out in the sun with my dog, Merc. He ran his hand over the dog's fur and then came inside to tell me that my dog was a living, breathing science project. Merc's white spots were more or less cool to the touch, but his black spots were very hot. Same dog, same body, same fur, but some of it was cool and some was hot.

The word *albedo* refers to the ability of an object to reflect radiant energy: shiny or white objects (like clouds or snowfields) reflect most of the energy that strikes them back into space; dark or black objects (like bare soil or blacktop pavement) absorb most of the energy that strikes them.

Here is how to play Merc's Albedo game. First, you'll need three or four people. If you all have different-colored hair you won't need anything else, but if you're all blonds or brunets, be sure you're wearing different colors — some light, some dark, some in between. Everybody has to be out in the sun for a while (at least 10 minutes) before you begin the game. One of you will be it and will be blindfolded. That person has to touch everyone else's head or back (or arm if you have different-colored skin) and guess who they are by how hot they feel. Blond heads will feel cooler than dark heads, and a black T-shirt will feel much hotter than a white one.

7

The Storm Puzzle

If you have ever been in a severe storm, you know that our system sometimes releases energy in scary, dangerous, and even devastating ways. The power of a hurricane or a tornado is not only scary, but awesome, too. Even normal-size thunderstorms, with their explosions of thunder and lightning, are reminders of the tremendous forces that create weather.

There is as much energy in a big thundercloud as in 10 bombs of the sort that devastated the Japanese city of Hiroshima during World War II (and that's almost small compared to the huge systems that generate tornadoes or hurricanes). Thunderheads are so dangerous, in fact, that even large commercial planes avoid the risk of flying into them.

In the early days of aviation, there was no way to dodge thunderstorms. But in the 1950s, United Airlines sent a DC-3 airplane named *Little Sir Echo* into the summer sky to develop a radar system that could detect and map thunderstorm activity. Once the system was completed, it was installed, one plane at a time, in United's fleet. A pilot flying into thunderstorms with the new system was able, for the first time, to pick up the storm on his radar and fly around it. Radar is now standard equipment on all commercial planes, but 30 years ago, when pilots were flying "by the seat of their pants" through thunderstorms, it was a miraculous new tool.

In 1959 a Marine Corps pilot, Lieutenant Colonel William H. Rankin, was attempting to fly over a large thunderstorm when his engine seized and he had to eject at 47,000 feet. For the next 40 minutes, dangling from his parachute, he was thrown violently around inside the screaming, churning cloud. After he finally came to earth and spent some time recovering from his injuries, he was able to furnish the world with an amazing account of the turbulence inside a thundercloud (or *cumulonimbus* cloud).

The forces at work inside a thunderstorm are fueled mostly by energy that is released when water vapor is converted into liquid water. In Chapter 6 we learned about the processes that transform and release energy, and now we will look at the end result of those processes in the weather that happens over the surface of our planet.

People used to think that storms developed in the sky right over their own heads, did whatever they were going to do, and then just melted back into the sky. Although there are isolated storms that work that way, most storms move as complete systems and may sweep over thousands of miles before finally losing strength.

Almost 250 years ago Benjamin Franklin, who was curious and observant enough to discover things by accident, found out that storms move from one place to another. The "accident" that happened was a storm coming just in time to ruin something he'd been looking forward to (that's probably happened to you, too). Mr. Franklin, who was very weatherwise and interested in everything that happened in the sky, was waiting for an eclipse of the moon that was supposed to happen on a certain night. A violent storm (which was actually the edge of a hurricane) swept into Philadelphia, where he lived, and blotted out the entire sky. A few days later he read in a newspaper that the eclipse had been visible in Boston, which is 260 miles northeast of Philadelphia, but that on the *next* night there had been a terrific storm in Boston.

Mr. Franklin figured the storm that hit Boston was the same one that had ruined his eclipse a few days earlier, and he concluded that storms actually moved from one place to another. He was able to prove his idea several years later, when he tracked a hurricane from North Carolina to New England. This discovery was like putting together the first two pieces of the storm puzzle. Then, about 80 years later, another American weather forecaster, William Redfield, found the next important piece.

Like all weatherwise people, Redfield was an enthusiastic observer of nature. He enjoyed going on cross-country hikes for hundreds of miles, and he recorded his observations in a journal. One of his hikes through Connecticut happened shortly after a hurricane had swept through the area, and as he walked, he noticed something very odd.

When he started out, he saw that hundreds of trees that had been blown down by the huge storm were all pointing toward the northwest. That made sense because, as he well remembered, the wind during the storm had been blowing from the southeast. But much to his surprise, after he had traveled to the other side of Connecticut, he saw that the downed trees there were pointing in the opposite direction, with their tops to the southeast. He arrived at the conclusion that the storm had been something like a gigantic whirlwind that moved from south to north, and he spent the next 10 years of his life tracking hurricanes to prove his theory.

Ben Franklin and William Redfield discovered two important things about storms: they move as complete systems over the surface of the earth, and, as they move, they spin in a counterclockwise direction. (If that counterclockwise spin rings a bell, it's because we found out in Chapter 3 that air in the northern hemisphere moves counterclockwise around areas of low pressure.) These were revolutionary discoveries, but it took a long time for someone to find and put together the next pieces of the storm puzzle.

In the first decades of the twentieth century a group of scientists in Norway, led by a man named Vilhelm Bjerknes, confirmed one of the most important principles of modern meteorology: air moves in large masses that are very different from each other (hotter or colder, wetter or dryer), and when these masses collide, they create weather disturbances.

Up until that time, meteorologists thought that, since storms always seemed to happen around low-pressure areas, it must be the low pressure that caused them. Bjerknes found out that it is the collision of warm and cold air masses that causes storms, and that a low-pressure area forms as part of the process.

In Chapter 3 we learned that in the midlatitude zones there is a band where warm air from the tropics collides with cold air from the poles. There is an actual boundary, like a belt all around the earth, where these air masses come together and form a *stationary front* ("stationary" because it doesn't move, and "front" because it's like the battle zone, or front, in a war). From time to time, a bulge of warm air pushes up into the cold air, kind of like a wedge. Both air masses begin to spin around the point of the wedge, and a low-pressure area is formed.

The whole rotating mass is called a *frontal system,* and it has both a *warm front* and a *cold front* in it. The best way to understand the process is to look at the picture below. You can see that the forward line of the wedge is where the warm air is lifting up and over the cold air. This is called a warm front. Meanwhile, at the back of the wedge, there's a boundary where cold air is pushing in and under the warm air, and this is called a cold front. Rain or snow happens at both edges, and the wedge of warmer air in between can be hundreds of miles wide.

Once a friend of mine named Duncan was riding his motorcycle from San Francisco to Boulder, Colorado, in the middle of the winter. There was a warm front ahead of him and a cold front behind him, and he managed to stay inside the wedge of warmer air between the two for almost the whole way. When he left San Francisco, there was a snowstorm about 200 miles in front of him, and another storm moving in behind him from the west. The one in front was at the *steering line* of the system, where the warm front was, and the one behind was at the *squall line,* where the cold front was.

After riding all day, Duncan began to catch up with the warm front, and he ended up, soaking wet and semifrozen, in a little mountain town in the middle of the night. He spent the night there, let the warm front get a little ahead of him and let the cold front catch up a little, and then continued on his way. Every time he got too close to the warm front, he stopped for coffee. He caught up with the storm again a few hours from Boulder, but this time, fortified by some homemade weather protection, he decided to keep going. He rode into Boulder with cut-up cardboard boxes wrapped around his arms and legs, got off his motorcycle, and let the warm front move past him for good. About a day later the cold front that was behind him blew through town, dropping a small amount of snow and pushing the temperature way below the motorcycle comfort zone.

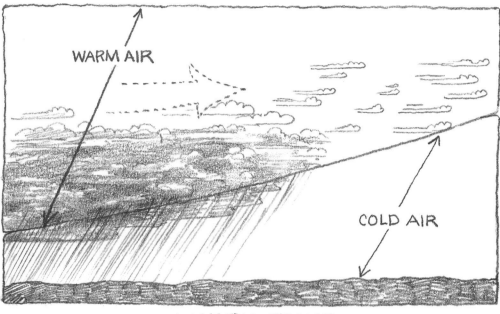

WARM AIR

COLD AIR

A WARM FRONT

The reason information about fronts is useful is that fronts usually behave in certain ways. If you understand how they work, you can make some predictions about the weather. For one thing, fronts move from the west to the east. They may move from the southwest to the northeast, or the northwest to the southeast, but either way the general flow is from west to east. (Even though the whole system is moving in an easterly direction, winds inside of it can come from other directions.) Another thing is that the cloud and precipitation patterns that happen at a warm front are different from those that happen at a cold front, and when you know the patterns, you can tell which one is coming.

If you have ever made plans according to a TV or radio weather forecast, and then had to change them when a storm blew in, you know that fronts don't always follow the rules. But still, most of them behave in a predictable manner. At a warm front, if the warm air that is riding up over the cold has plenty of moisture in it, then, as it is lifted up and over the cold air, it cools and the moisture in it condenses to form clouds. The first sign that a warm front is coming is often high, wispy (*cirrus*) clouds that show up a day or so before the front moves in on the ground.

As the warm front approaches, the clouds get thicker and lower until the whole sky is covered with a layer of gray *stratus* clouds, which can produce a period of overcast skies and rain or snow. In the United States, frontal activity is more likely to happen in the winter than in the summer, so warm fronts often bring snowstorms. If the warm air mass in a frontal system doesn't have enough moisture in it, it won't cause clouds or precipitation, and you might not even know that a warm front has passed.

Cold fronts are very different. In this case it is cold air that is pushing into warm air, and since cold air is heavier, it pushes up underneath and forces the warm air to rise very rapidly. This situation creates towering cumulonimbus clouds, and the squall line that announces a cold front is often a line of thunderclouds that bring rain or snow for a short period and then clear up. There is usually a quick drop in temperature at the same time.

Cold fronts are especially easy to recognize in hot summer weather, when there might be the sudden appearance of a line of thunderclouds and a rapid drop in temperature. It is often the squall line of a passing cold front that breeds tornadoes, so if you live in the "tornado belt," an important part of weatherwisdom is to know and recognize clues that announce the arrival of a strong cold front.

A COLD FRONT

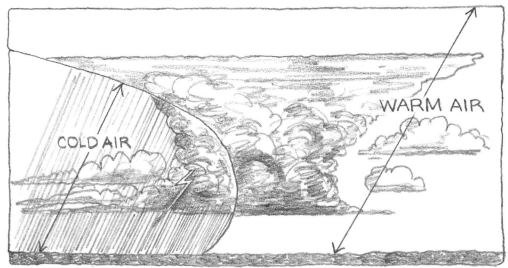

COLD AIR

WARM AIR

In the United States, warm, moist air from the Gulf of Mexico collides with cooler dry air moving across from the west, creating a perfect breeding ground for tornadoes. Because of this, the U.S. has the unhappy distinction of being the tornado capital of the world (up to 640 a year, compared to 60 a year in Great Britain and 10 a year in Italy).

Tornadoes are the most powerful storms we know of. They are so strong that no one has yet invented instruments that can survive in them long enough to measure their wind speed or barometric pressure. Tornadoes produce some of the strangest stories you've ever heard, and it isn't at all surprising that the events in *The Wizard of Oz* happened because of a tornado (in fact, if you want to see what a tornado looks like, that's a good movie to watch).

It's not unusual for a tornado to rip the feathers off chickens and leave them alive but looking pretty embarrassed. Train cars have been lifted off their tracks and carried 80 feet through the air before being dropped back down to the ground. Tornadoes are extremely dangerous, and much harder to predict than their big sisters, the hurricanes. But, like hurricanes, they breed only under special conditions.

It takes the collision of warm and cold air masses to create a tornado. The warm air is forced violently upward when it collides with a cold mass, and air flowing in from the sides gives the rapidly rising air a twist. Once rotation of the air inside a thundercloud has begun, a twirling funnel of air extends out of the bottom of the cloud toward the ground. When it contacts the ground, winds inside the funnel may be moving at up to 300 miles an hour.

By then, the rising and spinning air in the core of the tornado has created a suction so powerful that it can lift an entire truck up into the cloud. The extreme difference between air pressure inside the funnel and outside of it is enough to cause damage all by itself. The only bit of good news about tornadoes is that they don't last very long (but if you get in the way of one, that isn't very comforting).

Technology for forecasting tornadoes is improving, but we still cannot predict where and when a tornado will strike. However, though tornadoes can hit anytime, we do know that they are more likely to strike in the spring and early summer, and that they tend to happen in

the afternoon or early evening. Since they are often spawned at the squall line of a strong cold front, weather forecasters in tornado country pay close attention to frontal activity.

Before a tornado hits, black thunderclouds will sometimes take on a greenish tinge. It is often possible to see the beginning of the rotational movement in the clouds (like a slowly moving whirlpool) and, later, the funnel. A loud roaring noise means that the funnel is very close. If you have a barometer, you will see that there is a big drop in pressure. The best place to be is in the southwest corner of a cellar or basement (tornadoes generally move from southwest to northeast, so damage is usually greater on the northeast side). If you are outside (or in a mobile home), the best place to be is flat on your stomach in a ditch or ravine.

It is much easier to predict and track a hurricane than a tornado. For one thing, all hurricanes (or *typhoons,* as they are called if they happen in the Pacific) are born over warm, tropical oceans. And even though they travel hundreds of miles, because they are fueled by water vapor that is sucked up from the surface of a warm ocean, they cannot move far over land.

The combination of heat and moisture in the atmosphere over tropical oceans often creates a gathering of separate thunderstorms that may come together and become the seedling for a hurricane. If wind conditions are right and the seedling begins to spin, a strong low-pressure center develops and the separate thunderstorms become organized around it. As it spins faster, it is fed by the warm moist air that is being sucked up in the low-pressure center, and it becomes a full-fledged hurricane.

Hurricanes are the deadliest storms on earth not only because of their winds but also because of the *storm surge* that comes along with them. A storm surge is a huge wave of water, up to 40 feet high, that sweeps inland with a hurricane and destroys anything in its path. A big part of the work of the early warning system for hurricanes is to move

HURRICANE FORMING (OVERHEAD VIEW)

1. CLUSTER OF SEVERE STORMS

2. TROPICAL STORM

3. HURRICANE

people out of the way of the storm surge. Fortunately, hurricanes are now tracked by airplanes and satellites, and they no longer sneak up and catch us by surprise.

A very interesting time to watch weather on the television is during hurricane season, because the satellite pictures show you exactly how a hurricane develops and moves. The same thing is true of frontal systems, but the best time to watch them is in the winter, when temperature differences between polar and tropical air masses are greater. Here is an exercise that will help you read TV weather maps.

—— Reading a Weather Map ——

If you have ever seen a weather map, you probably noticed that it's covered with lines, squiggles, and symbols. Fortunately, most maps use the same lines, squiggles, and symbols to stand for the same weather events, so once you learn how to read one weather map, you can read them all. The trick, of course, is to find out what the various symbols mean. The map on the next page is a real weather map, and the key at the bottom shows the symbols and how they're used.

Some of the symbols on the map are decorated lines that show where the warm and cold fronts are. The key will tell you which kind of front is which. Low- and high-pressure areas show up in circular shapes that get bigger and bigger, like bull's-eyes (those are the thick, plain black lines). Some of the circular shapes cover so much area that only a small part of the circle shows up on the map.

The small circles with tails give information about cloud cover and wind speed and direction. The inside of the circle tells you how much of the sky is covered with clouds; the line coming out of the circle shows what direction the wind is coming from; and the little "feathers" sticking out of the line tell you how fast the wind is blowing. All of these things are explained in the key. (The black-flag symbol in the key — for winds of 50 knots and above — doesn't show up anywhere on this weather map, but you'll see it in the hurricane map in the next chapter.)

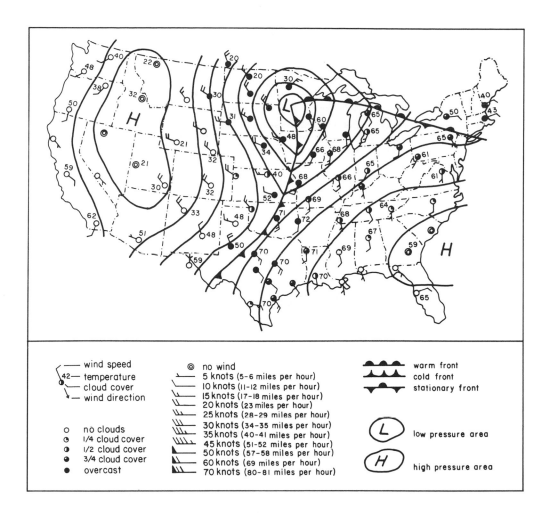

Take a careful look at the key, figure out what the symbols mean, and then see if you can answer these questions:

1. What state is under the center of the low-pressure area?
2. Where do you think precipitation from the warm front is falling?
3. What kind of precipitation do you think it is?
4. On the day this map was made, what was the weather like (including wind speed and direction) where you live?

Answers:
1. Minnesota
2. In the Great Lakes region
3. Snow near the center of the low and rain farther away from it

8

Keeping a Weather Eye Open

Sometimes when you aren't paying any attention to it, the weather sneaks up on you, pounces, and gives you the surprise of your life. If you aren't ready, it might cause you some inconvenience (like drenching you and your science project on the way home from school), or it might put you in real danger (like unleashing a flash flood through your campsite). Either way, though, weather surprises can be very unpleasant. The wonderful thing about weatherwisdom is that, if you have it, you are less likely to get caught by weather's "surprise attacks."

Although you may never have to use your wits in a weather emergency, it is also possible that you will find yourself in a situation where weatherwisdom makes a difference. Here are stories about two weatherwise children who figured out weather events before they happened and were able to save themselves and people around them from trouble.

74

Paquito lives on the beautiful mountainous island called Puerto Rico, which lies in the cool breezes of the trade winds. Puerto Rico is part of a chain of tropical islands in the Caribbean Sea. Paquito and his family live on the north coast, where the trade winds push wet air against the mountains until it lifts up, cools off, and drops its rain. Paquito's family has nearly always gotten its living from the sea, and Paquito himself has been a fisherman since he was a young boy. Living near the ocean — and floating on it day and night in a small boat — has sharpened his senses to the world around him, and he has studied the weather for as long as he can remember.

Even when Paquito first woke up before dawn on that crazy Monday (*"el lunes loco"* is what people on the island called it later), he knew that something was wrong. He listened with his eyes closed for a minute and then swung down out of his hammock and ran to the door. Don Frito, the ornery old rooster, had been crowing his head off — and that was right, but Paquito was hearing clucking sounds from under the house, and that was wrong. It meant that the hens had roosted under the house instead of up in the trees outside, and they only did that when a big storm was coming.

Paquito was so used to the birds' dawn racket that he usually didn't hear it, but this morning it was the silence that woke him. Not only was it quieter than usual outside, but as he went through the kitchen, Paquito realized that his mother was making coffee without the usual early-morning radio music. He stopped at the water tap outside the kitchen window to splash his face and then lifted his head to scan the sky. There were a few high, wispy fingers of cloud — very different from the small, puffy, cotton-ball clouds that made up the usual "trade wind sky."

While he was watching the sky, a frigate bird flew inland high over his head. He knew that frigate birds lived out at sea and only came inland to lay their eggs or to escape severe storms, so it began to look to Paquito as if very bad weather was on the way. His grandmother had long ago told him, and he had since found out for himself, that if spiders built their webs closer to the ground than usual, a bad storm was brewing. This morning most of the webs he found were near the ground.

These were all bad signs, but the high, wispy clouds were probably the worst. He had been thinking of the possibility of a big storm ever since he woke up, but when he saw those clouds, for the first time he thought, "hurricane." At least the radio would warn them if there was a hurricane in the area, and Paquito went back into the house to listen for a report. But his mother told him that everyone's electricity was out, so there wasn't any weather report. What a crazy time for this to happen! "I'm looking at clouds and spider webs and thinking about hurricanes, and our radio is out!"

Paquito went down to the shore to tell his father about the hurricane signs. He listed them one by one and included the fact that the waves were much bigger than usual, as if they were running before a storm. Paco, his father, had been repairing their small boat, and because he wasn't going out fishing in it that morning, he hadn't been paying much attention to the sky. Paco had great respect for his son's weatherwisdom, but he wasn't ready to move the whole family up to the hills, which was what he would need to do if there really was a hurricane on the way.

They decided to go talk to Paquito's old grandmother, the *abuelita* (which means "little grandma" in Spanish), who had taught him most of what he knew about the weather. The *abuelita* saw them coming and laughed. "Paquito, you've been gossiping with the chickens and the spiders this morning!" she said. Paquito laughed, too, because it was true that the bugs and animals had been telling him tales.

One of the *abuelita*'s most reliable weather signs was the fact that her arthritic fingers ached whenever the pressure dropped, and low pressure always means stormy weather. The *abuelita*'s fingers ached as they never had before, and she was certain, too, that the family should start moving inland. Between the two of them, Paquito and the *abuelita* convinced Paco that a hurricane was coming. They warned the village, and then they packed as much as they could carry and tied everything else down. Four hours after Paquito had awakened on *"el lunes loco,"* he and his family were in a cave just over the first low ridge of hills. It had clouded up and begun to rain as they were leaving their village, but by the time the hurricane struck, they were well over the high-water line and in the cave.

The strangest thing happened when the eye of the storm passed over them. Before then the wind had been whipping out of the northeast; some trees were blown completely down, and all of the palms were bent almost to the ground with their tops facing the southwest. Then, for almost half an hour, there was no wind at all. Paquito even had time to leave the cave and gather avocados for lunch. But when the wind started up again, it came from the opposite direction, and all the palm trees were blown the other way, with their tops on the ground facing the northeast.

When the hurricane finally left Puerto Rico, it passed over Hispaniola and Cuba before it veered to the northeast. It eventually passed over Florida, and finally went out to sea and died over the Atlantic Ocean.

The whole family (including Don Frito and most of the hens) survived the storm. After the events on *"el lunes loco,"* Paquito became known in the village as a weather forecaster, and even some of the old fishermen asked his advice from time to time. Thanks to Paquito's warning, and in spite of the radio blackout, no one in his village was killed in the hurricane.

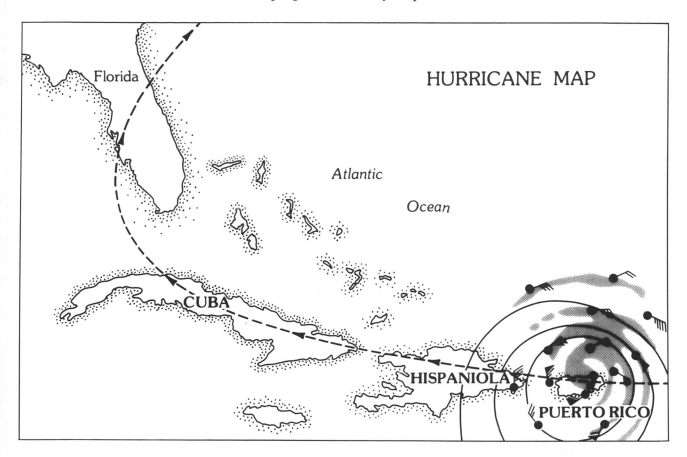

If you use what you learned in the last chapter about reading weather maps, you can find out more about Paquito's hurricane by looking at the hurricane map (above). The gray area shows where the heaviest rains were falling, and the flags, if you use the key on the weather map on page 73, tell you how fast and from what direction the wind was blowing. The hurricane map also shows you the path of the hurricane after it left Puerto Rico.

Sometimes extreme weather events trigger other sorts of problems. For example, too much precipitation falling too fast almost always causes trouble. Anyplace on the earth where there is snow and a surface for it to slide on (and that means most high mountain areas), avalanches can be a real hazard. Most avalanches happen during or right after a storm, so part of weatherwisdom for people in the mountains is learning about the weather conditions that produce avalanches.

Erin and her family live in an old mining town near Telluride, Colorado. Their cabin is high in the San Juan Mountains, and over the years, Erin has learned to love and appreciate the many moods of the mountains. She has also learned to respect them, especially after the winter of her twelfth birthday — the year of Dave's avalanche.

Everyone in Erin's family knows how to ski (even her four-year-old sister), because in the winter there is no other way to get to their cabin. Since she has skied to school and back most of her life, Erin is an avid weather watcher. She knows how to read the clouds and wind, she recognizes all the different types of snow, and she watches and understands the nightly weather forecasts on TV. She also keeps a notebook of her own observations, including the temperature, pressure, wind direction, wind speed, and cloud cover.

During Thanksgiving vacation when Erin was twelve, her older cousin, Josh, and his friend Dave, came to visit and to ski. They arrived on the first day of a three-day storm that ended up dumping 17 inches of new snow on top of the old, crusty "base." Even during the storm, Erin, Josh, and Dave skied every day, and Erin was careful to keep clear of any of the possible avalanche slopes. (Her father runs the ski school at Telluride, and he has made sure that everyone in the family, except four-year-old Becky, is an avalanche expert.)

Erin kept careful track of the snowfall during the storm and knew that it had dropped a little over one inch of snow per hour during the last 10 hours. That meant "red flag" avalanche conditions, especially since there was a strong wind out of the northwest during the last day of the storm. Both Josh and Dave were excellent skiers, so Erin kept her worries to herself but steered them clear of any danger areas.

The day after the storm dawned clear and cold, and the two visitors were ready to set out on their own. It was the last day of Thanksgiving vacation, and Erin had promised her mother she wouldn't ski until her book report was done. But she was still worried about avalanches, so she got out a topographic map and showed her cousin exactly which bowls and gullies to avoid.

She had a hard time convincing the boys that the avalanche danger was real and ended up having an argument with Dave because he wanted to ski exactly where she was telling him not to. (Why should he, an accomplished and experienced skier, take the advice of a twelve-year-old kid?) She turned to Josh in exasperation, and asked him to promise not to ski Turkey Basin, telling him that, just for today, the bowl up there was going to be deadly.

Before they left, Josh promised to avoid all of Erin's danger zones, and she tried to settle down to her book report. But she got more and more nervous, and before 15 minutes were up, she knew that she wouldn't be able to concentrate on her work. The problem was that Erin just didn't trust Dave not to do something dumb. She found her mother and little Becky upstairs in the loft and explained why she had to go out after them.

Erin packed her day pack, tied a shovel and some avalanche probes onto it "just in case," and set out with her dog toward Turkey Basin. The farther she went, the worse she felt, and she soon found herself skiing at racing speed. Following in Josh and Dave's tracks, it was clear that they were heading in the direction of Turkey Basin. In less than half an hour she had covered the distance that she figured it would take the boys closer to 45 minutes to go, and she reached the basin only a few minutes after they did.

Erin could see through the trees that Dave was about halfway down the bowl and Josh was standing close to the top. Just as Josh took off, the snow under his skis cracked in a jagged line all the way across the bowl and began to slide. Josh seemed to realize right away what was happening. "Avalanche!" he yelled, throwing his ski poles away from him. He struggled to stay on his feet and on top of the moving snow. Within seconds the cloud of snow had pulled Josh partway under, and Erin could see him "swimming" in the snow to stay on top.

When the tumbling cloud hit Dave, it covered him almost at once. Erin saw his yellow windbreaker tumble inside the cloud for a second, and then he disappeared. The snow continued to slide for almost a minute, and when it had settled, she looked for traces of the two skiers.

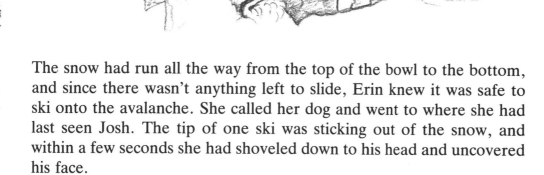

The snow had run all the way from the top of the bowl to the bottom, and since there wasn't anything left to slide, Erin knew it was safe to ski onto the avalanche. She called her dog and went to where she had last seen Josh. The tip of one ski was sticking out of the snow, and within a few seconds she had shoveled down to his head and uncovered his face.

She called her dog and ordered him to find Dave: "Where's Dave, Willie? Find Dave!" Willie began sniffing over the snow, and Erin skied to the base of the avalanche and started probing it with her avalanche probe. Before she had found anything, though, Willie started whining and digging furiously in the snow. Erin got there with her shovel and began digging, in horrible fear that by the time she found him, Dave wouldn't be breathing.

He was buried under 4 feet of snow, on his side, with his head pointing downhill. When she uncovered his head, his face looked gray, but he started breathing almost as soon as she broke the ice over his face. With the help of her dog, she had gotten to both of them in time. Nothing could have been a better reward for her years of studying weather and storms.

Both of these stories are about extreme weather events, and they show how important weatherwisdom can be. But everyday weather, though not as dramatic, can be just as important to you. By now your weather station is nearly complete, and with the next project you can finish it. If you really want to understand the weather, taking regular readings from your weather station and writing them down is an important step.

—————— Weather Station III ——————

The last two instruments you will make are for measuring the amount of moisture, or *humidity,* in the air (a *hygrometer*), and for indicating the direction of the wind (a weather vane).

HYGROMETER. To make this instrument you will need a piece of wood about 9 inches tall by about 4 inches wide (a scrap of 2 × 4, piece of plywood, etc.), a flat piece of plastic from a milk or water container, some glue that works on plastic and wood, 2 small nails, or brads, and 3 long strands of hair (if yours is short, you will have to ask someone to donate in the name of science).

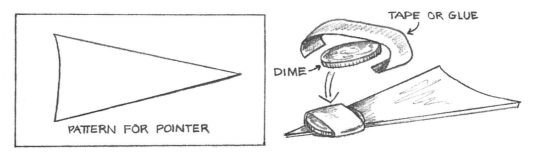

PATTERN FOR POINTER

TAPE OR GLUE

DIME

First you need to cut a pointer (about the same size and shape as the pattern) out of the flat piece of plastic. Use a pair of scissors that won't be ruined by cutting plastic.) The pointer will be like a needle on a gauge, with the pointed end indicating the humidity and the other end fastened to the wood. Tape or glue a dime to the end of the pointer (as shown in the picture above) to give it a little extra weight. Now put one of the brads through the wide end of the pointer and move it around until it makes a hole big enough so that the pointer spins easily on the brad. Pound the other brad into the upper right corner of the piece of wood, leaving at least one-fourth of it sticking out.

Glue the ends of the hairs to the pointer, just to the left of the nail hole (look at the picture to see where things go), and then nail the pointer onto the wood, about three-fourths of the way down the right side. Now pull the loose ends of the hairs up until the pointer is pointing straight to the left, and then wrap them around the base of the brad that you pounded into the top of the wood. Glue the ends of the hairs in place at the base of the brad.

When there is a lot of moisture in the air, the hairs will expand and the pointer will move down. When the air is dry, the hairs will become shorter and the pointer will move up. Make marks on the wood every day to show where the needle is pointing, and you will be able to tell whether the humidity is high, normal, or low. Add this information to your weather record each day.

WEATHER VANE. Everybody has seen weather vanes up on roofs of houses and barns, and most of us know that they tell us which way the wind blows. The one that you are going to make won't be very fancy, but it will work just fine. Because buildings and trees create strange air currents, the higher you put your weather vane, the better it will work. That means that you'll have to ask an adult to help you put it up after you have built it.

For this project you will need a wooden broom handle, a disposable aluminum baking dish, a piece of medium-soft wood (but not balsa) about a foot long and a half-inch square from a hobby shop, several nails, some strong glue, a washer, a small saw or a kitchen knife with a serrated edge, and some wire for mounting the weather vane when it is done.

First you need to prepare the foot-long wooden strip, or shaft, to make a swinging pointer. Use a small saw, or if you don't have one, a serrated kitchen knife, to cut a vertical slot into each end of the shaft, about a half-inch deep. Then measure and mark the exact center of the shaft, halfway between the two ends, and pound a nail into that point. Drive the nail most of the way through the shaft, and be sure the nail is going the same direction as the slots. Turn the shaft around on the nail until the hole is big enough for it to turn easily.

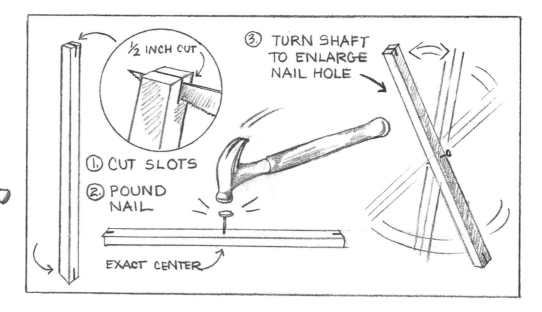

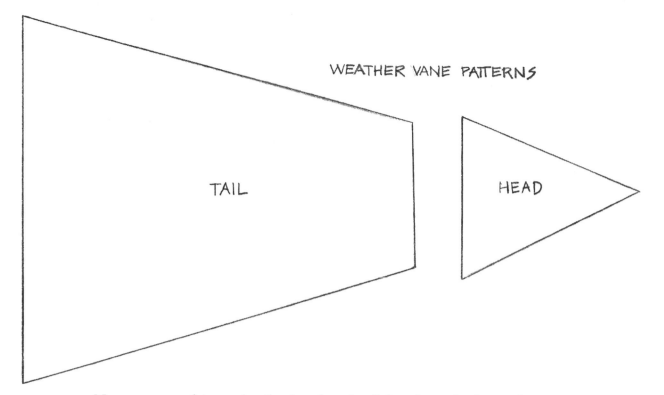

WEATHER VANE PATTERNS

TAIL

HEAD

Now you need to make the head and tail for the swinging pointer. Cut these pieces out of the aluminum baking dish, using the patterns above to get the right shape and size. (Again, be sure not to use anyone's good sewing scissors!) Stick the aluminum head into the slot at one end of the shaft and the tail into the other one, and glue them in place (use plenty of glue).

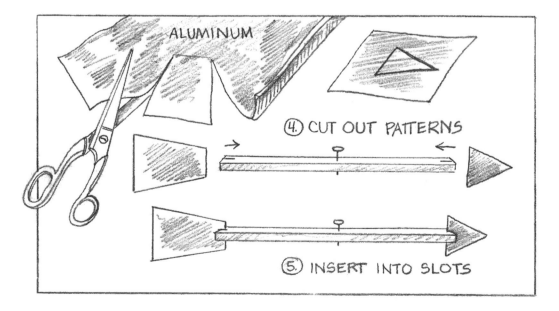

ALUMINUM

④ CUT OUT PATTERNS

⑤ INSERT INTO SLOTS

You will need some help to attach the swinging pointer to the broom handle. First, put the washer on top of the broom handle, and then put the shaft over it so that the nail will go down through the washer and into the handle of the broom. Drive the nail into the broom, leaving it loose enough for the pointer to turn around easily. The weather vane is finished, but mounting it may be the biggest part of the project.

6. NAIL SHAFT AND WASHER TO BROOM HANDLE

The best place to put the weather vane is on the side of a house, barn, or shed, so that it is sticking up above the roof line. If that isn't possible, try attaching it to the fence post next to the one that has your rain gauge on it. If you are mounting it on a fence post, wire the broom handle to the fence post in several places, so that the weather vane is very firmly tied to the post.

If you mount it on the side of a building, you will need a ladder and an adult to help. Almost all buildings have roofs that overhang the outside walls, and you'll have to mount the weather vane to the side of the overhang. There are many different roof constructions, so you may need some help to figure out the best way to mount the weather vane on your type of roof. The illustrations on the next page show some of the possibilities.

Once it is mounted, the pointer will swing into the wind so that the head is pointing in the direction that the wind is coming from. Use your Stonehenge model to tell you which direction is which, and record the wind direction every day with the rest of your daily observations.

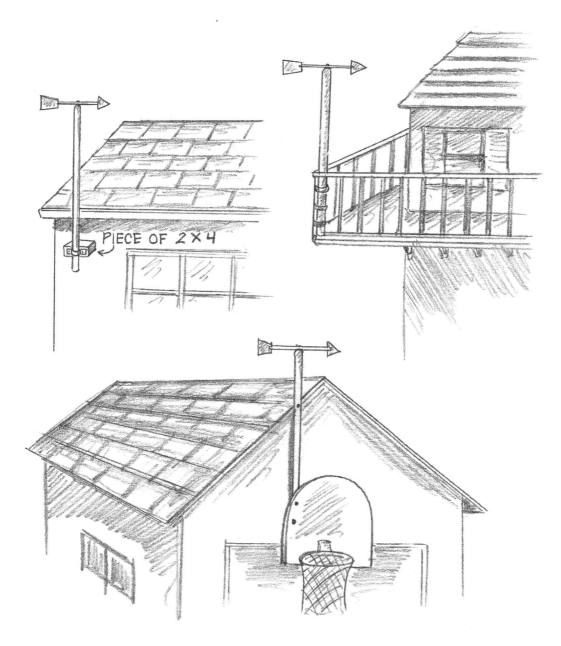

PIECE OF 2×4

9

Putting It All Together

By the time you get to the end of a book like this one, hundreds of facts have gotten loaded into your head. Luckily for you, one of the great talents of the human brain is its ability to sort through different tidbits of information, find how they are related, and put them together in patterns that make sense. It's like putting together a puzzle that has an endless number of pieces, and every once in a while, when a whole bunch of pieces come together at once, you see something that you have never seen before.

One of the reasons that people can be weatherwise, whether they have scientific technology and precise instruments or not, is that they are carrying around the greatest weather instrument known to human-kind, right in between their ears. Not only can it sort through old information, but it has the most amazing ability to notice new things, connect them with what it already knows, and find the hidden patterns in them.

If you had the right equipment and complete instructions, you could build a machine that would record all the information that your weather instruments collect. But a machine couldn't figure out what it means, and it couldn't glance up in the sky and connect the recorded information with what it sees, smells, hears, feels, and tastes. Even the most complicated computer program can only do what someone tells it to.

Whether or not you understand how low-pressure systems work, if you record the weather for several months, you might notice that every time the pressure falls, you're in for stormy weather. You have the ability to detect the patterns hidden in your weather record. Of course, the best combination is to understand what a low-pressure system is *and* to notice the weather patterns that seem to go along with it.

Some of the best patterns of all are hidden outside in the world around and the sky above you. The weatherwise children you've been reading about looked for and noticed weather signs of all kinds; things like animals, clouds, and bugs had become part of their weather-wisdom. A very important part of your own store of weather knowledge, then, will be your collection of local weather signs. Some of them you can learn from other people, and some of them you may figure out for yourself.

There are several weatherwise people in my family, and one of them is my father. He grew up on a farm in Colorado, and as a child, he spent a lot of time on the back of a horse. He herded cattle when he wasn't in school, and when he *was* in school, he got there by riding horseback. Either way, he was outside in the weather a lot, and understanding (and predicting) it got to be very important to him.

He noticed things about the wind: if it was blowing gently out of the south during the winter, that meant clear skies and bitter cold; if it swung around to the northeast during the fall or spring, that meant heavy, wet snow. He noticed things about the clouds: if cumulonimbus clouds built up over the Rocky Mountains to the west before 11 o'clock in the morning, there would probably be thundershowers in the afternoon; if the thunderclouds had a yellowish color, it would probably hail. And he noticed things about animals: calves and colts would become very frisky before a storm, and when birds lined up in rows on wire fences or telephone lines, autumn was coming and it was getting to be time for them to migrate south.

These are examples of things you can look for yourself or ask other people about. Birds can help you predict the weather, but they are like

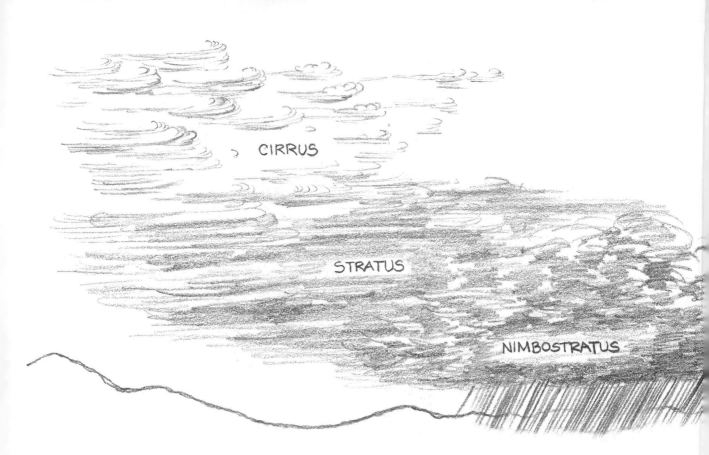

any other signs: they work only if you pay attention to them. Swallows, the small birds that have open, **V**-shaped tails, are good weather signs. They are amazing acrobats that eat while they're flying, and it's fun to watch them darting through the air, chasing after tiny little insects. Traditional weatherwisdom says that when swallows fly low, it is a sign of rain, and that is often true. When a cold front moves in, it forces the bugs down closer to the ground, so the swallows have to fly low to catch them. And, as you know, cold fronts often bring rain.

Some human beings (like Paquito's *abuelita*) are also weather "instruments." People who have arthritis, or have had injuries to their joints (knees, elbows, ankles, and so on), experience serious aching when the pressure drops. Unfortunately, it is a real pain to be a weather instrument, but since aching joints can be a reliable source of weather information, we might as well pay attention to them.

Some of the most obvious weather signs, of course, are clouds. There are many ways of identifying clouds, and if you don't want to learn someone else's system, you can make up one of your own. Some classification systems for clouds are very complicated, and others are simple. One of my cousins says there are two types of clouds: the ones

that look like animals and the ones that don't. Well, if you make up your own system, you might want it to be a little more complicated than that, but my cousin has the basic idea.

The real question is not so much what you call the clouds that look like animals, but what they mean. What kind of information are they giving you about the weather? For instance, now that you know something about how frontal systems work, you might be able to predict one by watching the clouds and checking the barometer in your weather station. You learned in Chapter 7 that clouds in a frontal system happen in a normal series of events, so if you can read the clouds, you will know what kind of weather to expect.

The first clouds you will see, up to a day or two ahead of the front, are very high, thin, wispy cirrus clouds. As the cirrus clouds become thicker, you will know that the steering line, or warm front, is getting closer. The clouds will keep getting thicker and lower until they cover the whole sky in a layer of stratus clouds.

When the stratus clouds become dark rain clouds (nimbostratus) and produce precipitation, then the warm front is at ground level. Rain or snow from the warm front may last a day or two, and then the sky will clear (or partially clear) up. After that a line of puffy cumulus clouds, followed by thunderclouds (cumulonimbus), will announce the cold front. Precipitation from a cold front is normally heavier but shorter-lasting than from a warm front. When the cold front passes, the sky will clear up again, but frontal systems often follow each other, so be sure to check your barometer. If it drops, another frontal storm is probably on the way.

Even though every front is different, there are some general rules that they all follow. If that weren't true, the job of predicting them would be much harder than it is. Isolated storms that develop in any local area are much harder to predict, because they depend on conditions that exist right there. Where I live, for instance, most of our winter storms are frontal, but in the summer, storms are usually isolated and local, so I have to know local weather signs and patterns to predict summer weather. Learning how to read clouds helps me do that.

Many of the old weather sayings are related to clouds. "Red sky at night, sailor's delight, red sky in the morning, sailors take warning." Well, where I live that isn't true (for one thing there isn't any water, and so, no sailors). A red sky at night means there are clouds in the west, and since most storms here usually come out of the west, if there are red clouds at sunset it means there's a storm on the way.

In New England, on the other hand, most bad storms come from the northeast (that happens when there's a low-pressure area to the south, and the counterclockwise flow of air around it brings wind into New England from the northeast), so if there are clouds to the west it means the storm has already passed. That's a good example of why you have to know local weather signs to understand your own weather.

Another old weather saying about clouds is "A ring around the moon means it's going to rain." That one is usually true if the barometer is falling at the same time, because the high-altitude cirrus clouds that make a halo around the moon are the ones that come ahead of a warm front. So if there's a halo around the moon, *and* the barometer is falling, the chances are good that it will rain in 18 to 48 hours. (Of course not all warm fronts bring rain, so you can't be sure of what will happen.)

One of the best ways to understand and learn to predict local weather (besides using your homemade weather station and learning about weather signs) is to watch the local weather report on television. Ever since the invention of satellite technology, we have had a view of our planet that couldn't even have been imagined a hundred years ago, and you can see the satellite view of the earth every evening on television. That view will confirm a lot of what you already know about the weather.

You can watch the clouds swirl in a counterclockwise direction around low-pressure areas, and it really seems as though you can see them sucking up moisture from the oceans and bringing it over land. You can see the bands of precipitation along storm fronts, and usually those fronts are marked with the warm- or cold-front symbols. In the summer, when there's not a great temperature difference between polar and tropical air masses, warm fronts may not even show up. But in the winter you can usually see both the warm and cold fronts, and watch them move, over a period of a few days, in an easterly direction.

The satellite picture will also show you that high-pressure areas usually bring clear weather, and low-pressure areas bring clouds and storms. Although there are always exceptions to weather rules, a general rule of thumb is "high and dry." You will discover the same thing yourself if you take readings at your own weather station.

Other than the satellite pictures, the TV weather report will give you just about the same information you get from your own weather station: temperature, humidity, wind direction, barometric pressure, and what they call "measurable precipitation." If you live very far from the nearest television broadcasting station, you will find out how much difference there is between your own weather and the weather in that city.

As you learn more about the weather, and especially if you are in a weather emergency, you'll find out for yourself how important it is to be prepared. Take the right kind of clothing with you when you leave home, particularly if you are going on a camping trip or a journey in your car. If you are traveling in your car through an area where snow-storms or any other extreme weather events are likely to happen, it could be very important to be prepared.

As you become more weatherwise you will notice things you've never seen before, and discover your own fascinating bits and pieces of weather knowledge. Like any other kind of wisdom, once you've got it, it's yours forever, and the next thing you know, someone will be asking *you* how to become weatherwise.

Glossary

Albedo
The amount of solar radiation reflected off a particular surface.

Atmospheric pressure
The force created by the weight of the atmosphere.

Autumnal equinox
September 22 or 23, one of the two times in the year when the sun is directly overhead at the equator, and day and night are of equal length all over the world. (Also called the fall equinox.)

Barometer
An instrument for measuring changes in atmospheric pressure.

Cirrus
A high-altitude, feathery type of cloud that often forms before a warm front.

Climate
The average long-term weather conditions in any particular region.

Cold front
A moving boundary between two air masses, where the cold mass is pushing up under the warm mass.

Condensation
The conversion of a gas to either liquid or ice.

Cumulonimbus
A towering thundercloud that sometimes brings severe weather and often occurs at a cold front.

Cumulus
A low-altitude, puffy white cloud.

Decomposition
The process of breaking down, or decaying.

Deflect
To turn to the side.

Dew point
The temperature at which vapor condenses into liquid.

Eclipse
A situation in which the sun is partly or totally hidden when the moon comes between it and the earth (a solar eclipse), or in which the moon is partly or totally hidden by the earth's shadow (a lunar eclipse).

Equatorial trough
A band of low pressure that encircles the earth around the equator.

Evaporation
The process of changing from a liquid to a gas.

High latitude
Those areas on the earth that are between the poles and about 55° north and south of the equator.

High pressure
A condition in which the weight of the atmosphere (at any particular place on the earth's surface) is greater than normal. This condition usually means clear, dry weather.

Humidity
A measurement of how much water vapor is in the air at any particular place.

Hydrologic cycle
The movement of Earth's water from the surface of the planet, through the atmosphere, and back down to the ground.

Hygrometer
An instrument for measuring the humidity, or water vapor content, of the air.

Low pressure
A condition in which the weight of the atmosphere (at any particular place on the earth's surface) is less than normal. This condition often brings cloudy skies and some sort of precipitation.

Midlatitude
Zones of latitude that extend between about 23° and about 55° north and south of the equator.

Molecule
The smallest particle that anything can be broken down to.

Nimbostratus
A low, widespread raincloud.

Ozone
An oxygen gas that forms a layer in the upper atmosphere and blocks out ultraviolet radiation from the sun.

Photosynthesis
The production of chemical energy by green plants, using carbon dioxide, water, and radiant energy from the sun.

Precipitation
Either liquid or frozen water that reaches the ground by falling through the atmosphere.

Sirocco
A strong desert wind blowing out of the Sahara into a low-pressure area over the Mediterranean Sea.

Solar radiation
Energy from the sun that is transmitted through space.

Squall line
The trailing edge of a frontal system, where the cold front is.

Stationary front
An unmoving boundary between two masses of air.

Steering line
The leading edge of a frontal system, where the warm front is.

Stratus
A type of low-altitude cloud that forms in a thick gray layer, often covering the entire sky at any one place.

Subtropical high
Either of two belts of high pressure that encircle the earth at about 30° north and south of the equator.

Summer solstice
June 21 or 22, the longest day of the year in the northern hemisphere and the shortest day of the year in the southern hemisphere.

Trade winds
Steady easterly winds that blow toward the equator from the northeast in the northern hemisphere and from the southeast in the southern hemisphere.

Ultraviolet radiation
A type of radiation from the sun that can be damaging to living beings.

Vapor
The gaseous state of any substance (for example, water vapor).

Vernal equinox
March 20 or 21, one of the two times in the year when the sun is directly overhead at the equator and day and night are of equal length all over the world. (Also called the spring equinox.)

Warm front
A moving boundary between two air masses, where the warm air rides up over the cold air.

Westerlies
Prevailing winds that blow out of the west over the midlatitude zones.

Winter solstice
December 21 or 22, the shortest day of the year in the northern hemisphere and the longest day of the year in the southern hemisphere.

Index